KU-167-674

The Microwave Cookbook

Jill Spencer

Hamlyn
London   New York   Sydney   Toronto

Acknowledgements
The author and publisher would like to thank the following for
their help in sponsoring photographs for this book
Alcan Polyfoil *pages 70–71*
Birds Eye Foods Limited *pages 18–19 and 110–111*
Buxted Advisory Service *page 11*
Colman's Mustard *page 35*
Corning Glass International SA Mfr *pages 58–59*
The Farmhouse English Cheese Federations *pages 86–87*
Jif Lemon Bureau *page 31*
Knorr *page 74*
Marmite *pages 38–39*

Other photographs kindly supplied by
American Long Grain Rice *pages 14 23 47 90 and 107*
Charbonnier Wines Counsel Limited *page 55* Gale's Honey
page 51 Knorr *page 95* M E A T *pages 43 and 99* Potato
Marketing Board *page 83* Taunton Cider Company Limited
page 79 Wines from Germany Information Service *page 62*

Microwave ovens kindly loaned by
Philips Electrical Limited
Moffat Cooker Division of Thorn Domestic Appliances
(Electrical) Limited
Photography by John Lee
Line drawings by Ann Rees

Published by
The Hamlyn Publishing Group Limited
London New York Sydney Toronto
Astronaut House Feltham Middlesex England

© Copyright The Hamlyn Publishing Group Limited 1978
All rights reserved. No part of this publication may be
reproduced, stored in a retrieval system, or transmitted, in any
form or by any means, electronic, mechanical, photocopying,
recording or otherwise, without the permission of The Hamlyn
Publishing Group Limited

ISBN 0 600 36282 5
Thirteenth impression 1984
Printed and bound by Graficromo s.a., Cordoba, Spain
Phototypeset by Tradespools Limited, Frome, Somerset

Contents

Useful facts and figures

Notes on metrication

Exact conversion from Imperial to metric measures does not usually give very convenient working quantities and so the metric measures have been rounded off into units of 25 grams. The table below shows the recommended equivalents.

Ounces	Approx g to nearest whole figure	Recommended conversion to nearest unit of 25
1	28	25
2	57	50
3	85	75
4	113	100
5	142	150
6	170	175
7	198	200
8	227	225
9	255	250
10	283	275
11	312	300
12	340	350
13	368	375
14	396	400
15	425	425
16 (1 lb)	454	450
17	482	475
18	510	500
19	539	550
20 (1¼ lb)	567	575

Note When converting quantities over 20 oz first add the appropriate figures in the centre column, then adjust to the nearest unit of 25. As a general guide, 1 kg (1000 g) equals 2·2 lb or about 2 lb 3 oz. This method of conversion gives good results in nearly all cases, although in certain pastry and cake recipes a more accurate conversion is necessary to produce a balanced recipe.

Liquid measures The millilitre has been used in this book and the following table gives a few examples.

Imperial	Approx ml to nearest whole figure	Recommended ml
¼ pint	142	150 ml
½ pint	283	300 ml
¾ pint	425	450 ml
1 pint	567	600 ml
1½ pints	851	900 ml
1¾ pints	992	1000 ml (1 litre)

Spoon measures All spoon measures given in this book are level unless otherwise stated.
Can sizes At present, cans are marked with the exact (usually to the nearest whole number) metric equivalent of the Imperial weight of the contents, so we have followed this practice when giving can sizes.
Flour Plain flour is used in the recipes, unless specified otherwise.
Stock Use boiling water poured on to a stock cube.

Notes for American and Australian users

In America the 8-oz measuring cup is used. In Australia metric measures are now used in conjunction with the standard 250-ml measuring cup. The Imperial pint, used in Britain and Australia, is 20 fl oz, while the American pint is 16 fl oz. It is important to remember that the Australian tablespoon differs from both the British and American tablespoons; the table below gives a comparison. The British standard tablespoon, which has been used throughout this book, holds 17·7 ml, the American 14·2 ml, and the Australian 20 ml. A teaspoon holds approximately 5 ml in all three countries.

British	American	Australian
1 teaspoon	1 teaspoon	1 teaspoon
1 tablespoon	1 tablespoon	1 tablespoon
2 tablespoons	3 tablespoons	2 tablespoons
3½ tablespoons	4 tablespoons	3 tablespoons
4 tablespoons	5 tablespoons	3½ tablespoons

An Imperial/American guide to solid and liquid measures

Solid measures

IMPERIAL	AMERICAN
1 lb butter or margarine	2 cups
1 lb flour	4 cups
1 lb granulated or castor sugar	2 cups
1 lb icing sugar	3 cups
8 oz rice	1 cup

Liquid measures

IMPERIAL	AMERICAN
¼ pint liquid	⅔ cup liquid
½ pint	1¼ cups
¾ pint	2 cups
1 pint	2½ cups
1½ pints	3¾ cups
2 pints	5 cups (2½ pints)

Note When making any of the recipes in this book, only follow one set of measures as they are not interchangeable.

American terms

The list below gives some American equivalents or substitutes for terms and ingredients used in this book.

BRITISH/AMERICAN
cling film/saran wrap
greaseproof paper/wax paper
foil/aluminum foil
kitchen paper/paper towels
liquidise/blend
mince/grind
packet/package
polythene/plastic

Introduction

For those embarking on microwave cookery for the first time, I am sure you will find it as exciting and rewarding as I have done. It is a completely different way of cooking, so it is important to read and understand the introductory chapter before launching into the recipes.

All the recipes were created and tested in the Hamlyn test kitchen. I would like to thank Bridget Jones for her invaluable help in compiling these recipes and assistance on the photography sessions. The scope of food that can be cooked in a microwave is endless, as you will discover when you start using it yourself. Even your favourite recipes can be adapted for the microwave. With the busy pace of everyday life, time becomes more valuable to everyone. This is where the microwave oven plays an important role. Once you have mastered the art of microwave cookery, you will never look back!

There are many models of microwave oven available, and new ones are coming on to the market all the time. It is impossible to keep up to date with the latest trends, as the whole concept of microwave cookery is moving very quickly. The expansion of the market is probably due to more working wives leading a very active life. To the next generation of housewives a microwave oven will become as much a necessity as the freezer is to the housewife of today.

I would like also to thank Jenny Webb, a well-known authority on microwave ovens, for her help and advice in compiling this book.

I hope you will enjoy your new adventure into the world of microwave cooking as much as I have done.

Jill Spencer

All about microwave ovens

The microwave oven

All microwave ovens consist of the same basic unit. Depending on the model, additional features may include variable power settings, defrost and stay-hot controls, browning elements, turntables and temperature probes. Cookers which combine microwave and conventional cooking facilities are also available.

Variable power settings

A variable power control enables you to slow down the rate of cooking by reducing the amount of microwave energy which reaches the food. This facility is particularly useful when cooking delicate foods or the tougher cuts of meat. However, there are no standard controls, so the number of settings and the way in which they are presented varies widely between different makes of oven. They may be expressed as a numerical scale, ranging from 1–5 or 1–10, or as low, medium and high, or even just as roast, bake or reheat. The manufacturer's booklet will explain the controls of your particular oven.

To avoid any confusion between the settings of different makes of oven, all the recipes in this book were tested on the full power output of a 600 Watt oven. If your oven has variable power control use the highest setting or full power. If the output of your oven is lower than 600 Watts, you should increase the cooking time; if the output is higher, you should decrease the cooking time or use a lower setting.

A selection of utensils suitable to use in a microwave oven

How the microwave oven works

(a)   The *plug* is inserted into the socket and the energy begins to flow.
(b)   The *power transformer* increases the voltage and supplies the components in the high voltage circuit.
(c)   The high voltage *rectifier and capacitor* changes the alternating voltage to undirectional voltage.
(d)   The *magnetron* converts the electrical energy into electro-magnetic or microwave energy.
(e)   The *waveguide* guides the microwave energy towards the oven cavity.
(f)   The *wave stirrer* distributes the microwaves evenly throughout the oven.
(g)   The *oven cavity* has metallic walls, ceiling and floor which reflect the microwaves.
(h)   The *oven door* is fitted with special seals to ensure that there is the minimum of microwave leakage. At least one cut-out device is incorporated in the door so that the microwave energy is automatically switched off when the door is opened.
(i)   The *oven shelf* on which the food or container is placed.

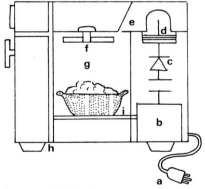

Cross-section of a microwave oven

How the microwave oven cooks or heats food

Microwaves can react in one of three ways when used with different substances. They are either
(a)   reflected *or*
(b)   transmitted *or*
(c)   absorbed.
(a) Microwaves are *reflected* by metal or aluminium foil, just as a mirror will reflect light. The oven cavity is made of metal so that the waves are reflected

Microwaves being reflected

7

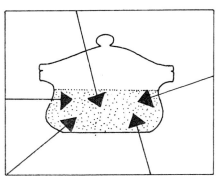

Microwaves being transmitted through a casserole dish

on to the food. It is therefore important to remember *not to use metal containers* in the oven as the microwaves would be reflected back, avoiding contact with the food.

(b) Microwaves are *transmitted* through substances such as glass, china, ceramics, paper and some plastic, just as light passes through a window. Certain glass containers and plastics should only be used for short time heating, whilst the other types of containers are the most suitable for microwave cooking.

(c) Microwaves are *absorbed* by food and liquid. The microwaves penetrate about 2.5–3.5 cm/1–1½ inches into the food, after which the heat is transferred by conduction.

The microwaves cause the molecules in the food to agitate, producing friction, which creates heat enabling the food to cook quickly.

Safety factors

All microwave ovens are fitted with safety devices ensuring the minimum of microwave leakage. The door is designed so that the microwave energy cuts off immediately it is opened. Some models are designed with drop-down doors; it is important not to stand heavy dishes on these, or even lean on them, as the alignment could be damaged.

Always remember to switch off the oven at the socket outlet, when not in use. With some ovens, if the control switch is accidentally turned on when the microwave is empty, the magnetron could be damaged.

When cleaning the microwave oven, do not allow the cleaning agent to soil or accumulate around the door seal, as this could prevent a tight seal when the door is closed. Never hang damp tea-towels on the oven door.

Do not attempt to use the oven if it becomes damaged, or try to repair it yourself. Always contact a qualified engineer.

Care and maintenance

Never use an abrasive cleaner to clean the interior of the oven, as it can scratch the metallic walls. Do not use aerosols either, as these may penetrate the internal parts of the oven. Simply wipe over with a cloth wrung out in soapy water and rinse with a clean cloth, or follow the manufacturer's instructions. Any persistent smells can be eliminated by heating a cup of lemon juice and water in the microwave.

Cooking utensils

The range of cooking utensils that can be used in the microwave oven is wide. In fact the choice is probably wider than when cooking in a conventional oven. It is, however, important to remember a few basic rules. *Always avoid metal dishes, metal baking trays, stainless steel dishes, foil dishes, cast-iron casseroles, dishes trimmed with metallic designs, dishes that have a certain amount of metal actually in the glaze or composition, glassware saucepans with metal screws or handles, metal ties on frozen foods and foil-lined freezer bags.* It is sometimes permissible to use small pieces of aluminium foil to protect wing tips of poultry or any parts of food that may cook more quickly, provided the foil does not come into contact with the oven walls. Always read the manufacturer's instruction booklet first, as individual microwave ovens do vary in exactly what is allowed.

China and pottery dishes
Use any ovenproof dishes or containers that you would normally use in a conventional oven, but if using a pottery dish check that it is not porous. Also

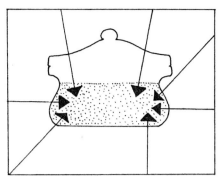
Microwaves being absorbed by food

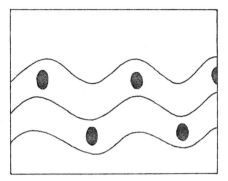
Molecules in food being agitated

remember to avoid using dishes trimmed with a metallic design. If you are using the same dish to cook and serve the food, remember that the dish will become hot as it absorbs heat from the food.

Glassware
Ovenproof glassware such as measuring jugs, basins and mixing bowls are ideal for the microwave, provided there are no metal trims or handles with screws.

Paper
Paper plates, cups, paper kitchen towels and napkins are all suitable for use in the microwave, particularly for reheating purposes and short time cooking. Check plates with a wax coating as they are inclined to melt! Food with a high liquid content, e.g. casseroles, will cause a paper plate to become soggy on reheating. Paper kitchen towels are ideal for cooking fatty foods, e.g. bacon, as they absorb the fat. They are also useful for covering food to prevent any spitting.

Plastics
Only the rigid plastic containers are suitable for the microwave. They should be confined to reheating purposes rather than prolonged cooking. If you are in doubt try a simple test – half-fill a container with water and bring to the boil in the microwave. Check at intervals that the container is still intact.

Plastic wrap
Cling film or freezer film is invaluable for covering dishes. Great care must be taken when removing the film, as trapped steam may cause a burn. It is advisable to pierce the film at intervals before cooking.

Plastic bags
Bags such as boil-in-bags, freezer bags and cook-bags may be used provided there are no metal ties. Use elastic bands or string to secure the bags, but make sure they are loosely tied to allow the steam to escape.

Wooden bowls
These are only suitable for short reheating purposes, e.g. when heating bread rolls.

Microwave accessories

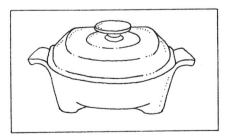
Microwave browning dish

The microwave browning dish
The microwave browning dish helps overcome the problem of browning food in the standard microwave oven. Its primary function is to brown meats, fish and poultry, although it can also be used successfully for cooking eggs and frying sandwiches.

It is a glass-ceramic dish with feet, designed so that the base of the dish does not come into contact with the base of the microwave. The outer side of the base is coated with a special light grey coating which absorbs the microwave energy. The empty dish is preheated in the microwave, the base becomes hot and changes colour. This dish can be used for casseroles, without the pre-heating period, provided the entire base is covered with the food. The pre-heating time of the dish varies according to the type of food being cooked and the output of the oven, so always follow the manufacturer's instructions. Do check that your particular model of microwave oven permits the use of this special dish. Corning Glass International is just one of the companies to manufacture this type of dish.

Microwave/freezer containers
Lakeland Plastics are now producing a range of microwave/freezer containers. These are manufactured from a selection of polythene and polystyrene, with the ability to withstand extreme temperatures, enabling the containers to be used more than once, and to take food in the container straight from the freezer to microwave.

Microwave cooking terms

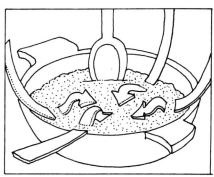

Stirring food to bring food in centre to the outer edges

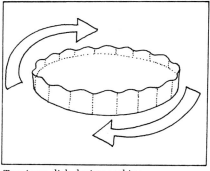

Turning a dish during cooking

Frozen food being defrosted in (below) too large a dish and (bottom) correct-sized dish

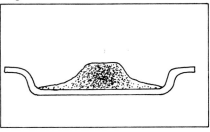

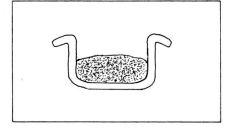

Stirring
The stirring of food is necessary in some recipes to obtain an even distribution of heat throughout, e.g. casseroles, soups, sauces, etc. As the microwaves cook the exposed outer edges of the food first, stirring helps to distribute the heat more evenly.

When stirring, remove the dish from the oven and stir the contents so that the inside food is moved to the outer edges of the dish, and vice versa.

Rearrangement and turning of food
When it is not possible to stir the food, the food must be rearranged in the microwave, for the same reason. This applies to dishes such as crème caramel, crème brûlée, etc.

If using individual dishes, it is necessary to rearrange the positions during cooking, so they can all cook evenly. A large dish, e.g. a cheesecake, will simply require turning during cooking.

Standing time
All food continues to cook to a certain degree once removed from the microwave oven, so it is sometimes necessary to have a standing period, to allow the heat to penetrate to the centre, e.g. a joint of meat. (See chart on page 61.) Sometimes the standing time comes in between the cooking times, e.g. a cheesecake requires a standing period as the mixture cannot be stirred, the dish can only be rotated. The standing time allows the heat to transfer naturally into the cooler centre of the food.

With smaller items such as vegetables the time between being removed from the microwave and being served is sufficient for heat transference. The denser the food the longer the standing time.

Defrosting frozen food in the microwave
The freezer and the microwave oven are natural partners. Frozen food can be taken from the freezer and put straight into the microwave oven, provided it is not in a foil container or a freezer bag lined with foil, and all the metal fastenings have been removed.

Defrosting in the standard microwave oven needs more attention than in a microwave with an automatic defrosting system, as the defrosting times and the standing times have to be alternated manually. The standing time allows the heat to be conducted into the centre of the frozen food, without actual cooking taking place. If food was defrosted without standing times, it would be unevenly thawed.

For defrosting times of meat (see page 61), chicken (see page 61), and convenience foods (see page 123).

If you have to transfer a block of frozen food to a different container for defrosting, choose a container to fit the shape of the frozen food. If the dish has too wide a surface area, the outside of the food will defrost, covering the base of the dish, and this will cook while the centre of the food remains frozen.

Defrosting a chicken for Rolled galantine of chicken (page 56)

Factors influencing microwave cooking

Starting temperatures
The colder the food when put into the microwave oven, the longer cooking time is required; so allowances must be made if using food straight from the refrigerator or freezer.

Density
The denser the food, the longer it will take to cook.

Shapes
Always aim for uniform shapes, especially with joints of meat. If one end of the joint is much thinner, this will obviously cook more quickly than the denser part of the joint. However, there are some joints which are never uniform, e.g. a leg of lamb. To overcome this problem, it is a good idea to bone and stuff the joint or bone and tie it into a neat shape. If your microwave oven permits the use of foil, then protect the thinner part of the leg with foil, and this will slow down the cooking time on the covered part.

Poultry should always have the legs and wings well tucked into the body. If these protrude then they will cook well in advance of the rest of the bird.

Frozen casseroles are normally an ideal shape to allow even defrosting.

Timing
The timing is probably the most crucial part of microwave cookery and it will often take a while to adjust to it. Each manufacturer provides a guide to timing for their particular model, as the levels of microwave energy vary with the different makes of oven. Always read the instructions carefully.

Remember it is better to undercook than to overcook. Undercooked food can always be rectified, but once overcooked the food becomes dehydrated and cannot be saved.

Unlike conventional cooking, the microwave cooking time increases with any additional items in the oven; for example, two mugs of coffee will take longer than one mug.

Cooking time is also affected by the shape and size of the cooking utensil used. If you are going to use utensils different from those stipulated in the recipes, remember to watch the timing carefully.

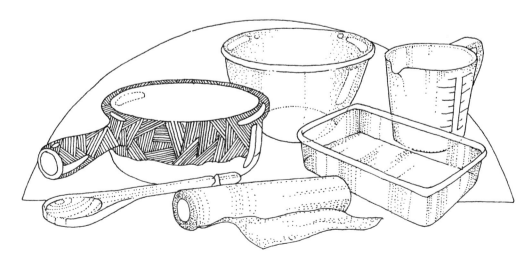

Information for using the recipes

As microwave ovens have produced a completely new concept in the world of cookery, it is important to read the chapter 'All about microwave ovens' before trying out the microwave-tested recipes in the book. It will make it easier for you to understand and enjoy trying the recipes.

All the recipes in this book were created and tested using a standard microwave oven with an output of 600 watts. Check the output of your oven and adjust the timing accordingly, using the times stated in the recipes as a guide. If your microwave oven has an output higher than 600 watts, the timings are going to be slightly shorter. If the output is below 600 watts, then the cooking time will be longer.

In each recipe the size and shape of utensil used has been given, also the total microwave cooking time and number of servings; so all the relevant information is there at a glance.

The utensils used have been kept to basic, everyday equipment usually found in any kitchen; glass measuring jugs, ovenproof mixing bowls, basins and casserole dishes.

If the food requires covering, then it is specified in the recipe. Cling film, freezer film, greaseproof paper and kitchen paper are all suitable.

It is worth remembering to go easy on the seasonings, as flavours can become accentuated. The shorter cooking time does not allow the seasoning to be readily absorbed, thus making it more concentrated.

When a recipe refers to stock, use boiling water poured onto a stock cube. If the stock is allowed to cool before being used, the cooking time will need to be increased.

And lastly, do refer to the manufacturer's instruction booklet for details about your particular microwave oven.

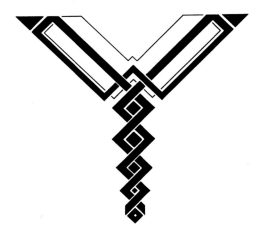

Soups and starters

Home-made soups are delicious cooked in the microwave. They can be prepared in advance and then reheated in the microwave when required. Always remember that food cooked or reheated in the microwave becomes extremely hot, so allow the soup to cool slightly before serving.

In emergencies canned soups can be reheated actually in the soup bowl, thus reducing washing up! Dried packet soups can be made and cooked in an ovenproof pudding basin.

Pâté is always popular, and is easy to cook in the microwave. Keep it in a refrigerator for up to 3 days or freeze until required.

Spinach soup

Illustrated on pages 18–19

Utensil: 2.25-litre/4-pint (U.S. 5-pint) ovenproof mixing bowl
Microwave cooking time:
   12 minutes

Serves: 4

METRIC/IMPERIAL	AMERICAN
25 g/1 oz butter	2 tablespoons butter
25 g/1 oz flour	¼ cup all-purpose flour
450 ml/¾ pint milk	2 cups milk
300 ml/½ pint hot chicken stock	1¼ cups hot chicken stock
½ teaspoon nutmeg	½ teaspoon nutmeg
1 tablespoon grated onion	1 tablespoon grated onion
salt and freshly ground black pepper	salt and freshly ground black pepper
1 (227-g/8-oz) packet frozen chopped spinach, thawed	1 (8-oz) package frozen chopped spinach thawed
double cream to swirl	heavy cream to swirl

Place the butter in the mixing bowl and melt in the microwave for 1 minute. Stir in the flour until well mixed, then gradually add the milk, stock, nutmeg, onion and seasoning, whisking well. Cook in the microwave for 7 minutes, whisking 3 times to prevent lumps forming. Add the spinach and mix well. Cook for a further 4 minutes in the microwave. Allow to cool slightly before liquidising. Reheat in the microwave if necessary. Swirl cream into the soup just before serving.

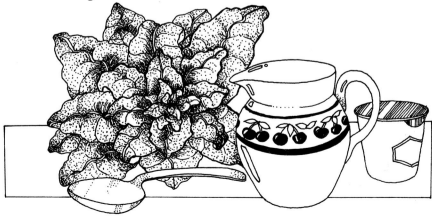

Chicken rice salad (page 94)

Bouillabaisse

Utensil: 1.75-litre/3-pint (U.S.
    4-pint) casserole dish
Microwave cooking time:
    14 minutes

Serves: 4

METRIC/IMPERIAL	AMERICAN
1 tablespoon oil	1 tablespoon oil
1 small onion, finely chopped	1 small onion, finely chopped
1 clove garlic, crushed	1 clove garlic, crushed
1 (226-g/8-oz) can tomatoes	1 (8-oz) can tomatoes
900 ml/1½ pints hot stock	3¾ cups hot stock
¼ teaspoon curry powder	¼ teaspoon curry powder
1 tablespoon tomato purée	1 tablespoon tomato paste
salt and freshly ground black pepper	salt and freshly ground black pepper
2 tablespoons chopped parsley	3 tablespoons chopped parsley
225 g/8 oz white fish, cut into bite-size pieces	½ lb white fish, cut into bite-size pieces
225 g/8 oz peeled prawns	1 cup peeled shrimp
1 (150-g/5¼-oz) can mussels	1 (5¼-oz) can mussels

Place the oil, onion and garlic in the casserole dish and cook in the microwave for 2 minutes. Stir in all the remaining ingredients, except the prawns and mussels, and cook in the microwave for 11 minutes, stirring twice during cooking. Add the prawns and mussels and continue to cook in the microwave for a further 1–2 minutes. Adjust the seasoning and allow to stand for a few minutes before serving.

Sweetcorn soup

Illustrated on pages 18–19

Utensil: 2.25-litre/4-pint (U.S.
    5-pint) ovenproof mixing bowl
Microwave cooking time: 8 minutes

Serves: 4

METRIC/IMPERIAL	AMERICAN
15 g/½ oz butter	1 tablespoon butter
1 medium onion, finely chopped	1 medium onion, finely chopped
50 g/2 oz bacon, chopped	2 oz bacon slices, chopped
15 g/½ oz cornflour	2 tablespoons cornstarch
300 ml/½ pint milk	1¼ cups milk
2 (170-g/6-oz) packets frozen sweetcorn, thawed	2 (6-oz) packages frozen corn kernels, thawed
300 ml/½ pint hot chicken stock	1¼ cups hot chicken stock
salt and freshly ground black pepper	salt and freshly ground black pepper

Place the butter, onion and bacon in the mixing bowl and cook in the microwave for 1 minute. Blend the cornflour and milk together and pour on to the bacon and onion. Cook in the microwave for 4 minutes, stirring twice during cooking. Whisk the sauce and add the sweetcorn, reserving a little for garnish, and stock. Return to the microwave for 3 minutes. Allow to cool slightly then liquidise the soup. Adjust the seasoning and reheat in the microwave if necessary. Garnish with reserved sweetcorn.

Cauliflower soup

Illustrated on pages 18–19

Utensils: 2.25-litre/4-pint (U.S. 5-pint) ovenproof mixing bowl, cook-bag
Microwave cooking time: 16 minutes

Serves: 4

METRIC/IMPERIAL
50 g/2 oz butter
1 onion, finely diced
2 tablespoons flour
750 ml/1¼ pints hot chicken stock
1 (339-g/12-oz) packet frozen cauli-flower florets
salt and freshly ground black pepper
Garnish:
2 tablespoons single cream
chopped parsley

AMERICAN
¼ cup butter
1 onion, finely diced
3 tablespoons all-purpose flour
3 cups hot chicken stock
1 (12-oz) package frozen cauliflower florets
salt and freshly ground black pepper
Garnish:
3 tablespoons light cream
chopped parsley

Place the butter and onion in the mixing bowl and cook in the microwave for 2 minutes. Stir in the flour, then pour in the stock and return to the microwave for 3 minutes. Place the frozen cauliflower in a cook-bag, secure loosely with an elastic band and cook in the microwave for 9 minutes, turning 3 times. Add the cauliflower florets to the sauce and cook in the microwave for 2 minutes. Allow to cool slightly then liquidise or sieve the soup. Adjust the seasoning and reheat in the microwave if necessary. Just before serving, stir in the cream and chopped parsley.

French onion soup

Utensil: 2.25-litre/4-pint (U.S. 5-pint) ovenproof mixing bowl
Microwave cooking time: 5 minutes

Serves: 4

METRIC/IMPERIAL
50 g/2 oz butter
350 g/12 oz onions, thinly sliced
2 tablespoons flour
generous litre/2 pints hot beef stock
salt and freshly ground black pepper
3 tablespoons sherry

AMERICAN
¼ cup butter
12 oz onions, thinly sliced
3 tablespoons all-purpose flour
5 cups hot beef stock
salt and freshly ground black pepper
¼ cup sherry

On a conventional cooker, melt the butter in a medium-sized saucepan. Add the onions and cook until brown, then stir in the flour to absorb most of the butter.

Gradually stir in the beef stock and seasoning. Transfer the soup to the mixing bowl. Cook in the microwave for 5 minutes. Stir in the sherry and allow to stand for a few minutes before serving.
Note: In order to obtain a good rich brown colour to this soup, it is necessary to fry the onions initially on the conventional cooker.

Spinach soup (page 15), Cauliflower soup (page 17) and Sweetcorn soup (page 16)

Minestrone soup

Utensil: 2.25-litre/4-pint (U.S. 5-pint) ovenproof mixing bowl
Microwave cooking time:
  23 minutes

Serves: 4

METRIC/IMPERIAL
1 tablespoon oil
1 carrot, sliced
1 stick celery, sliced
1 onion, chopped
1 potato, peeled and chopped
1 clove garlic, crushed
900 ml/1½ pints hot ham stock
25 g/1 oz spaghetti, broken into pieces
1 (226-g/8-oz) can tomatoes
1 leek, shredded
Garnish:
grated Parmesan cheese
chopped parsley

AMERICAN
1 tablespoon oil
1 carrot, sliced
1 stalk celery, sliced
1 onion, chopped
1 potato, peeled and chopped
1 clove garlic, crushed
3¾ cups hot ham stock
1 oz spaghetti, broken into pieces
1 (8-oz) can tomatoes
1 leek, shredded
Garnish:
grated Parmesan cheese
chopped parsley

Place the oil, prepared vegetables and garlic into the mixing bowl and cook in the microwave for 3 minutes. Stir well and add the stock and spaghetti, then cook in the microwave for 13 minutes, stirring twice during cooking. Add the tomatoes and leek and cook for a further 7 minutes in the microwave, stirring once. Allow to stand for a few minutes before serving. Garnish with Parmesan and chopped parsley.

Stilton soup

Utensil: 2.25-litre/4-pint (U.S. 5-pint) ovenproof mixing bowl
Microwave cooking time:
  8 minutes

Serves: 4

METRIC/IMPERIAL
1 tablespoon oil
1 small onion, finely chopped
1 tablespoon flour
300 ml/½ pint milk
600 ml/1 pint hot chicken stock
salt and freshly ground black pepper
1 bay leaf
pinch ground mace, nutmeg and
  cayenne pepper
225 g/8 oz Stilton cheese,
  crumbled
150 ml/¼ pint single cream

AMERICAN
1 tablespoon oil
1 small onion, finely chopped
1 tablespoon all-purpose flour
1¼ cups milk
2½ cups hot chicken stock
salt and freshly ground black pepper
1 bay leaf
pinch ground mace, nutmeg and
  cayenne pepper
½ lb Stilton or other blue cheese,
  crumbled
⅔ cup light cream

Place the oil and onion in the mixing bowl and cook in the microwave for 2 minutes. Stir in the flour then add all the remaining ingredients except the Stilton cheese and cream. Cook in the microwave for 5 minutes, stirring once. Add the cheese, reserving a little for garnish. Return to the microwave for 1 minute. Allow to cool slightly then liquidise or sieve the soup. Reheat in the microwave if necessary. Stir in the cream and sprinkle with the reserved Stilton.

Lentil and bacon soup

Utensil: 2.25-litre/4-pint (U.S. 5-pint) ovenproof mixing bowl
Microwave cooking time: 13 minutes

Serves: 4

METRIC/IMPERIAL	AMERICAN
100 g/4 oz lentils	½ cup lentils
900 ml/1½ pints hot ham stock	3¾ cups hot ham stock
4 rashers lean bacon, chopped	4 Canadian bacon slices, chopped
1 onion, finely chopped	1 onion, finely chopped
2 sticks celery, chopped	2 stalks celery, chopped
salt and freshly ground black pepper	salt and freshly ground black pepper
pinch cayenne pepper	pinch cayenne pepper
2 tablespoons chopped parsley	3 tablespoons chopped parsley

Soak the lentils overnight and then drain. Place the stock, bacon, onion, celery, seasoning and drained lentils in the ovenproof mixing bowl and cook in the microwave for 13 minutes, stirring twice during cooking. Allow to cool slightly then liquidise or sieve the soup. Adjust the seasoning and stir in the chopped parsley, reheat in the microwave if necessary.

Broccoli soup

Utensil: 1.5-litre/2½-pint (U.S. 3-pint) round ovenproof dish
Microwave cooking time: 8½–9 minutes

Serves: 4

METRIC/IMPERIAL	AMERICAN
1 small onion, finely chopped	1 small onion, finely chopped
25 g/1 oz butter	2 tablespoons butter
25 g/1 oz flour	¼ cup all-purpose flour
600 ml/1 pint hot chicken stock	2½ cups hot chicken stock
1 (226-g/8-oz) packet frozen broccoli, thawed and roughly chopped	1 (8-oz) package frozen broccoli, thawed and roughly chopped
salt and freshly ground black pepper	salt and freshly ground black pepper
pinch freshly ground nutmeg	pinch freshly ground nutmeg
300 ml/½ pint milk	1¼ cups milk

Place the onion and butter in the round dish and cook in the microwave for 2 minutes. Stir in the flour, then add the stock, chopped broccoli, reserving a little for the garnish, and seasonings. Cook in the microwave for 6 minutes, stirring twice during cooking. Allow to cool slightly then liquidise or sieve the soup. Adjust the seasoning and pour in the milk. Reheat in the microwave for ½–1 minute. Allow to stand a few minutes before serving. Garnish with the reserved broccoli.

Leek and potato soup

Utensils: cook-bag, 1-litre/2-pint (U.S. 2½-pint) ovenproof pudding basin, 2.25-litre/4-pint (U.S. 5-pint) ovenproof mixing bowl
Microwave cooking time: 16 minutes

Serves: 4

METRIC/IMPERIAL	AMERICAN
450 g/1 lb leeks, washed and sliced	1 lb leeks, washed and sliced
2 medium potatoes, peeled and diced	2 medium potatoes, peeled and diced
750 ml/1¼ pints milk	3 cups milk
1 chicken stock cube	1 chicken bouillon cube
150 ml/¼ pint boiling water	⅔ cup boiling water
salt and freshly ground black pepper	salt and freshly ground black pepper

Place the leeks and potatoes together in a cook-bag. Seal loosely with an elastic band or freezer tape and cook in the microwave for 10 minutes.

Heat the milk in the pudding basin in the microwave for 3 minutes and add to the leeks and potatoes in the mixing bowl. Stir in the stock cube and boiling water. Cook in the microwave for 3 minutes, cool slightly before liquidising or sieving the soup. Season to taste. Reheat in the microwave if necessary.

Creamy onion soup

Utensils: 3.5-litre/6-pint (U.S. 7½-pint) ovenproof mixing bowl, 300-ml/½-pint (U.S. 1¼-cup) glass measuring jug
Microwave cooking time: 16 minutes

Serves: 4

METRIC/IMPERIAL	AMERICAN
25 g/1 oz butter	2 tablespoons butter
450 g/1 lb onions, chopped	1 lb onions, chopped
1 tablespoon flour	1 tablespoon all-purpose flour
600 ml/1 pint hot chicken stock	2½ cups hot chicken stock
salt and freshly ground black pepper	salt and freshly ground black pepper
1 tablespoon chopped parsley	1 tablespoon chopped parsley
300 ml/½ pint milk	1¼ cups milk

Place the butter in the mixing bowl and melt in the microwave for 1 minute. Add the onions and cook in the microwave for a further 3 minutes. Stir in the flour then carefully mix in the chicken stock, seasoning and parsley, return to the microwave for 10 minutes.

Heat the milk in the measuring jug in the microwave for 2 minutes and add to the soup. Sieve or liquidise; reheat if necessary in the microwave oven and serve.

Tomato and horseradish soup

Utensil: 2.25-litre/4-pint (U.S. 5-pint) ovenproof mixing bowl
Microwave cooking time: 13 minutes

Serves: 4

METRIC/IMPERIAL	AMERICAN
25 g/1 oz butter	2 tablespoons butter
100 g/4 oz onion, finely chopped	1 cup finely chopped onion
25 g/1 oz flour	¼ cup all-purpose flour
450 g/1 lb tomatoes, skinned and chopped	1 lb tomatoes, skinned and chopped
600 ml/1 pint hot chicken stock	2½ cups hot chicken stock
salt and freshly ground black pepper	salt and freshly ground black pepper
3 teaspoons creamed horseradish	3 teaspoons creamed horseradish
3 tablespoons tomato purée	¼ cup tomato paste
pinch ground mace	pinch ground mace
Garnish:	Garnish:
4 tablespoons double cream	⅓ cup heavy cream
1 teaspoon creamed horseradish	1 teaspoon creamed horseradish

Place the butter in the mixing bowl and melt in the microwave for 1 minute. Add the onion and cook for 2 minutes. Stir in the flour and tomatoes, gradually add the chicken stock, seasoning, creamed horseradish, tomato purée and mace. Cook in the microwave for 10 minutes. Allow to cool slightly then sieve or liquidise. Garnish with swirls of double cream mixed with the creamed horseradish.

Mussel paella (page 92), Rice and vegetable salad (page 93)

22

Summer soup

Illustrated on front jacket

Utensils: cook-bag, 3.5-litre/6-pint
  (U.S. 7½-pint) ovenproof mixing
  bowl, 600-ml/1-pint (U.S. 2½-cup)
  glass measuring jug
Microwave cooking time:
  15 minutes

Serves: 4

METRIC/IMPERIAL	AMERICAN
225 g/8 oz potatoes, diced	1⅓ cups diced potato
50 g/2 oz onion, chopped	½ cup chopped onion
300 ml/½ pint hot chicken stock	1¼ cups hot chicken stock
1 lettuce, shredded	1 lettuce, shredded
salt and freshly ground black pepper	salt and freshly ground black pepper
pinch ground mace	pinch ground mace
600 ml/1 pint milk	2½ cups milk
Garnish:	Garnish:
4 tablespoons double cream	⅓ cup heavy cream
chopped mint	chopped mint

Place the potatoes, onion and stock in the cook-bag and seal loosely with an elastic band or freezer tape. Cook in the microwave for 5 minutes then place in the mixing bowl. Add the lettuce and seasonings to the potato mixture.

Heat the milk in the measuring jug in the microwave for 3 minutes then add to the soup and continue to cook in the microwave for 7 minutes. Liquidise or sieve the soup and serve hot or cold. Swirl the cream on top and sprinkle with chopped mint.

Artichoke soup

Utensils: cook-bag, 2.25-litre/
  4-pint (U.S. 5-pint) mixing
  bowl, 300-ml/½-pint (U.S. 1¼-cup)
  glass measuring jug
Microwave cooking time:
  19 minutes

Serves: 4

METRIC/IMPERIAL	AMERICAN
450 g/1 lb Jerusalem artichokes, peeled and sliced	1 lb Jerusalem artichokes, peeled and sliced
1 small onion, finely chopped	1 small onion, finely chopped
2 tablespoons lemon juice	3 tablespoons lemon juice
25 g/1 oz butter	2 tablespoons butter
2 tablespoons flour	3 tablespoons all-purpose flour
600 ml/1 pint hot chicken stock	2½ cups hot chicken stock
300 ml/½ pint milk	1¼ cups milk
salt and freshly ground black pepper	salt and freshly ground black pepper

Place the artichokes, onion, lemon juice and butter in the cook-bag. Seal loosely with an elastic band or freezer tape and cook in the microwave for 8 minutes.

Turn the artichoke mixture into the mixing bowl and stir in the flour. Carefully stir in the stock and cook in the microwave for 9 minutes, stirring 4 times during cooking.

Allow to cool slightly then liquidise or sieve the soup. Heat the milk in the measuring jug in the microwave for 2 minutes and stir into the soup. Taste and season the soup before serving.

Chicken liver pâté

Utensils: 1.5-litre/2½-pint (U.S. 3-pint) round ovenproof dish, 600-ml/1-pint (U.S. 2½-cup) glass measuring jug
Microwave cooking time: 8 minutes

Serves: 4

METRIC/IMPERIAL	AMERICAN
25 g/1 oz butter	2 tablespoons butter
1 tablespoon oil	1 tablespoon oil
1 clove garlic, crushed	1 clove garlic, crushed
1 medium onion, finely chopped	1 medium onion, finely chopped
350 g/12 oz chicken livers, washed and dried	12 oz chicken livers, washed and dried
salt and freshly ground black pepper	salt and freshly ground black pepper
freshly ground nutmeg	freshly ground nutmeg
1 tablespoon brandy	1 tablespoon brandy
100 g/4 oz butter	½ cup butter
Garnish:	Garnish:
lemon slices	lemon slices
cress	cress

Place the butter, oil, garlic and onion in the dish and cook in the microwave for for 3 minutes, stirring once during cooking. Add the chicken livers and seasonings, continue to cook in the microwave for 4 minutes, stirring twice. Stir in the brandy, cool slightly and liquidise until smooth. Place in 4 ramekin dishes and smooth the tops.

Place the butter in the jug and melt in the microwave for 1 minute or until melted. Pour over the individual pâtés and place a lemon slice in the butter. Chill until set and garnish with cress.

Farmhouse terrine

Utensils: 20-cm/8-inch round ovenproof pie dish, 0.75-litre/1–1¼-pint (U.S. 1½-pint) ovenproof soufflé dish
Microwave cooking time: 15 minutes

Serves: 4

METRIC/IMPERIAL	AMERICAN
100 g/4 oz ox kidney, chopped	¼ lb beef kidney, chopped
225 g/8 oz lamb's liver, chopped	½ lb lamb liver, chopped
225 g/8 oz lean pork, chopped	1 cup chopped lean pork
1 small onion, finely chopped	1 small onion, finely chopped
5 rashers streaky bacon, derinded	5 bacon slices, derinded
2 bay leaves	2 bay leaves
50 g/2 oz fresh breadcrumbs	1 cup fresh soft bread crumbs
salt and freshly ground black pepper	salt and freshly ground black pepper
pinch basil	pinch basil
1 clove garlic, crushed	1 clove garlic, crushed
1 egg, beaten	1 egg, beaten

Place the chopped offal, meat and onion in the pie dish and cook in the microwave for 5 minutes, stirring once during cooking. Stretch the bacon rashers using the back of a knife. Place the bay leaves on the base of the soufflé dish. Line the dish with the bacon rashers.

Mix the meats with the remaining ingredients and place in the lined dish, smoothing the surface with a knife. Cover with cling film or greaseproof paper and cook in the microwave for 10 minutes. Allow to stand for 5 minutes. Cover with a clean piece of greaseproof paper and place a heavy weight on a saucer or small plate on top. Allow to cool then refrigerate overnight. Turn out carefully. Serve with French bread and a salad.

Asparagus mousse

Utensil: 600-ml/1-pint (U.S. 2½-cup)
 glass measuring jug
Microwave cooking time:
 2–2½ minutes

Serves: 4–6

METRIC/IMPERIAL
1 (340-g/12-oz) can green asparagus
  spears
15 g/½ oz softened butter
15 g/½ oz flour
2 eggs, separated
15 g/½ oz gelatine
150 ml/¼ pint chicken stock
salt and freshly ground black pepper
pinch cayenne pepper
1 teaspoon lemon juice
150 ml/¼ pint double cream, whipped
Garnish:
lemon slices
cucumber slices

AMERICAN
1 (12-oz) can green asparagus
  spears
1 tablespoon softened butter
2 tablespoons all-purpose flour
2 eggs, separated
2 envelopes gelatin
⅔ cup chicken stock
salt and freshly ground black pepper
pinch cayenne pepper
1 teaspoon lemon juice
⅔ cup heavy cream, whipped
Garnish:
lemon slices
cucumber slices

Drain the juice from the asparagus into the measuring jug and combine with the butter and flour. Cook in the microwave for 2–2½ minutes, whisking once during cooking. Remove from the microwave and whisk well to remove any lumps. Allow to cool slightly then stir in the egg yolks.

Using the conventional cooker, dissolve the gelatine in the chicken stock in a saucepan over a low heat. Stir into the sauce. Chop the asparagus and stir into the sauce with seasonings and lemon juice. When on the point of setting, whisk the egg whites and fold into the sauce with the whipped cream. Pour into a wetted 1-litre/2-pint (U.S. 2½-pint) mould. Chill until set.

When required, dip the mould quickly into hot water and turn out. Garnish with lemon and cucumber slices.

Egg mousse

Utensil: 2.25-litre/4-pint (U.S. 5-
 pint) ovenproof mixing bowl
Microwave cooking time: 5 minutes

Serves: 4

METRIC/IMPERIAL
25 g/1 oz butter
1 clove garlic, crushed
3 tablespoons flour
300 ml/½ pint milk
4 hard-boiled eggs, chopped
2 eggs, separated
15 g/½ oz gelatine
2 tablespoons hot water
Garnish:
quartered hard-boiled eggs
watercress sprigs

AMERICAN
2 tablespoons butter
1 clove garlic, crushed
4 tablespoons all-purpose flour
1¼ cups milk
4 hard-cooked eggs, chopped
2 eggs, separated
2 envelopes gelatin
3 tablespoons hot water
Garnish:
quartered hard-cooked eggs
watercress sprigs

Melt the butter in the mixing bowl in the microwave for 1 minute. Add the garlic and stir in the flour. Gradually add the milk, whisking well, and return to the microwave for 4 minutes. Whisk the sauce 4 times during cooking and again very well at the end of the cooking time.

Add the chopped hard-boiled eggs and egg yolks to the sauce and cool slightly. Dissolve the gelatine in the hot water, add to the sauce and leave in a cool place until half set. Whisk the egg whites until they form stiff peaks then fold into the half set mixture. Pour into a lightly oiled 1.5-litre/2½-pint (U.S. 3-pint) mould and leave to set in a cool place.

Turn out on to a suitable serving dish and garnish with quartered hard-boiled eggs and sprigs of watercress.

Serve with Melba toast.

26

Smoked haddock pâté

Utensil: 1.75-litre/3-pint (U.S. 4-pint) round casserole dish
Microwave cooking time: 5 minutes

Serves: 4

METRIC/IMPERIAL	AMERICAN
450 g/1 lb smoked haddock fillets, skinned	1 lb smoked haddock fillets, skinned
2 tablespoons finely chopped onion	3 tablespoons finely chopped onion
225 g/8 oz cream cheese	1 cup cream cheese
salt and freshly ground black pepper	salt and freshly ground black pepper
Garnish:	Garnish:
lemon wedges	lemon wedges
parsley	parsley

Cut the fish into chunks and place in the casserole dish together with the onion. Cook in the microwave for 5 minutes, stirring twice.

Cool and liquidise the fish with the cream cheese. Taste and season before pressing into individual ramekin dishes or a large serving dish. Chill until firm and garnish before serving.

Grapefruit with vermouth

Utensil: kitchen paper
Microwave cooking time: 2 minutes

Serves: 4

METRIC/IMPERIAL	AMERICAN
2 tablespoons white vermouth	3 tablespoons white vermouth
2 tablespoons clear honey	3 tablespoons clear honey
2 grapefruit	2 grapefruit
Garnish:	Garnish:
mint leaf	mint leaf

Mix together the vermouth and honey. Halve the grapefruit and loosen the segments then carefully spoon the vermouth mixture over them.

Heat two halves at a time in the microwave on a double thickness of kitchen paper, allowing 1 minute for each pair. Half turn the grapefruit after 30 seconds. Serve hot garnished with a mint leaf.

Smoked mackerel crumble

Utensils: 4 (11-cm/4½-inch) individual ovenproof quiche dishes, 1-litre/2-pint (U.S. 2-pint) ovenproof pudding basin
Microwave cooking time: 6 minutes

Serves: 4

METRIC/IMPERIAL	AMERICAN
100 g/4 oz smoked mackerel fillets, skinned	¼ lb smoked mackerel fillets, skinned
2 tablespoons roughly chopped onion	3 tablespoons roughly chopped onion
2 eggs	2 eggs
150 ml/¼ pint milk	⅔ cup milk
50 g/2 oz Double Gloucester cheese, grated	½ cup grated cheese
1 tablespoon chopped fresh mixed herbs	1 tablespoon chopped fresh mixed herbs
75 g/3 oz crunchy peanut butter	6 tablespoons crunchy peanut butter
100 g/4 oz crisps and savoury biscuits, crushed	2 cups crushed potato chips and crackers
Garnish:	Garnish:
lemon slices	lemon slices
parsley sprigs	parsley sprigs

Liquidise the mackerel, onion, eggs, milk and cheese together. Stir in the herbs and divide the mixture between the 4 quiche dishes. Cook two at a time in the microwave allowing each pair 2 minutes.

Melt the peanut butter in the pudding basin in the microwave for 2 minutes then add the crumbs and mix well. Top the cooked fish with the crumb mixture and garnish with the lemon slices and parsley sprigs before serving.

Coquilles Saint Jacques

Utensils: 1-litre/2-pint (U.S. 2½-pint) round ovenproof dish, 600-ml/1-pint (U.S. 2½-cup) glass measuring jug
Microwave cooking time: 8½–9½ minutes

Serves: 2

METRIC/IMPERIAL	AMERICAN
15 g/½ oz butter	1 tablespoon butter
1 small onion, finely chopped	1 small onion, finely chopped
100 g/4 oz button mushrooms, sliced	1 cup sliced button mushrooms
150 ml/¼ pint dry white wine	⅔ cup dry white wine
4 scallops, washed and quartered	4 scallops, washed and quartered
1 teaspoon lemon juice	1 teaspoon lemon juice
2 tablespoons chopped parsley	3 tablespoons chopped parsley
salt and freshly ground black pepper	salt and freshly ground black pepper
bay leaf	bay leaf
15 g/½ oz butter	1 tablespoon butter
15 g/½ oz flour	2 tablespoons all-purpose flour
3 tablespoons single cream or milk	¼ cup light cream or milk
2 tablespoons dried breadcrumbs	3 tablespoons dry bread crumbs
Garnish:	Garnish:
lemon wedges	lemon wedges
parsley sprigs	parsley sprigs

Place the butter and onion in the dish and cook in the microwave for 3 minutes. Stir in the mushrooms, wine, scallops, lemon juice, parsley, seasoning and bay leaf. Cook in the microwave for 4 minutes, stirring once. Remove and discard the bay leaf.

Place the butter in the measuring jug and melt in the microwave for 30 seconds. Stir in the flour and mix into a smooth paste. Strain the liquor from the scallops on to the butter and flour mixture together with the cream and stir well. Pour this sauce on to the scallops and place in 2 scallop shells or individual dishes. Sprinkle with breadcrumbs and return to the microwave for 1–2 minutes. Garnish with lemon wedges and parsley sprigs.

Baked avocado with shrimps

Utensil: 600-ml/1-pint (U.S. 2½-cup) glass measuring jug
Microwave cooking time: 3½ minutes

Serves: 4

METRIC/IMPERIAL	AMERICAN
150 ml/¼ pint milk	⅔ cup milk
7 g/¼ oz butter	½ tablespoon butter
1 tablespoon flour	1 tablespoon all-purpose flour
½ (212-g/7½-oz) can shrimps, drained	½ (7½-oz) can shrimp, drained
pinch cayenne pepper	pinch cayenne pepper
salt and freshly ground black pepper	salt and freshly ground black pepper
few drops lemon juice	few drops lemon juice
2 teaspoons tomato purée	2 teaspoons tomato paste
2 ripe avocado pears	2 ripe avocados
Topping:	Topping:
1–2 tablespoons fresh breadcrumbs	1–2 tablespoons fresh soft bread crumbs

Place the milk in the measuring jug and heat in the microwave for 30 seconds. Mix the butter with the flour then whisk gradually into the milk. Return to the microwave for 1 minute, or until thickened. Add the shrimps, cayenne pepper, seasoning, lemon juice and tomato purée.

Cut the avocado pears in half and remove the stones. Brush the cut surface with a little lemon juice to prevent discoloration. Pile the shrimp filling in the centre of each avocado and sprinkle with breadcrumbs. Place the avocado pear halves in a circle on a sheet of kitchen paper and return to the microwave for 2 minutes, stopping after 1 minute to alter the position of the avocado halves.

Fish dishes

Fish cooked in the microwave retains all its natural flavour and nutrients. Cook-bags have proved very successful for cooking fish, especially whole fish such as trout.

If you are cooking a large piece of fish, try and arrange it into a uniform shape by tucking any thin parts, such as the tail, underneath. This will prevent the thinner parts overcooking.

Be careful not to overcook fish as it will toughen and dry out. Always undercook slightly, as the fish will continue to cook in its own heat, once removed from the oven.

Soused mackerel

Utensil: 2.25-litre/4-pint (U.S. 5-pint) deep oblong casserole dish
Microwave cooking time: 16 minutes

Serves: 4

METRIC/IMPERIAL
100 g/4 oz onion, sliced
150 ml/$\frac{1}{4}$ pint vinegar
150 ml/$\frac{1}{4}$ pint water
2 bay leaves
$\frac{1}{4}$ teaspoon salt
freshly ground black pepper
4 mackerel, cleaned and boned
Garnish:
lemon wedges
watercress

AMERICAN
4 oz onion, sliced
$\frac{2}{3}$ cup vinegar
$\frac{2}{3}$ cup water
2 bay leaves
$\frac{1}{4}$ teaspoon salt
freshly ground black pepper
4 mackerel, cleaned and boned
Garnish:
lemon wedges
watercress

Place the onion in the casserole dish and pour over the vinegar and water. Add the bay leaves, salt and freshly ground black pepper.

Place 2 mackerel in the liquid and cook in the microwave for 8 minutes, turning the fish 4 times during cooking. Remove the fish from the cooking liquid and cook the second pair of mackerel for approximately 8 minutes. (The second pair of fish may not take quite as long as the first pair since the cooking liquid will have already have been heated.) Serve the fish cold, garnished with lemon wedges and watercress.

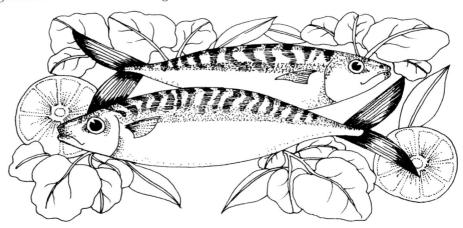

Kedgeree

Illustrated opposite

Utensils: 1.5-litre/2½-pint (U.S. 3-pint) shallow oblong ovenproof dish, 1.75-litre/3-pint (U.S. 4-pint) round casserole dish
Microwave cooking time: 22 minutes

Serves: 4

METRIC/IMPERIAL	AMERICAN
450 g/1 lb smoked haddock fillets	1 lb smoked haddock fillets
1 tablespoon lemon juice	1 tablespoon lemon juice
600 ml/1 pint boiling water	2½ cups boiling water
2 tablespoons chopped parsley	3 tablespoons chopped parsley
25 g/1 oz butter	2 tablespoons butter
1 onion, finely chopped	1 onion, finely chopped
175 g/6 oz long grain rice	¾ cup long grain rice
1 bay leaf	1 bay leaf
3 hard-boiled eggs, chopped	3 hard-cooked eggs, chopped
salt and freshly ground black pepper	salt and freshly ground black pepper
Garnish:	Garnish:
chopped parsley	chopped parsley
lemon slices	lemon slices

Place the fish in the oblong dish together with the lemon juice, boiling water and parsley. Cook in the microwave for 4 minutes, turning the dish once. Remove the fish and reserve the stock. Skin and flake the fish, removing any bones.

Heat the butter in the casserole dish in the microwave for 1 minute then add the onion and cook in the microwave for 2 minutes. Add the rice and bay leaf; pour over the fish stock and cook in the microwave for a further 15 minutes or until the liquid is absorbed.

Remove the bay leaf then mix in the fish and hard-boiled eggs. Season with salt and freshly ground black pepper. Garnish with parsley and lemon slices.

Paupiettes of plaice in wine sauce

Utensils: 1-litre/2-pint (U.S. 2½-pint) round shallow ovenproof dish, 1-litre/2-pint (U.S. 2½-pint) ovenproof basin
Microwave cooking time: 7 minutes

Serves: 4

METRIC/IMPERIAL	AMERICAN
8 plaice fillets, skinned	8 flounder fillets, skinned
150 ml/¼ pint white wine	⅔ cup white wine
150 ml/¼ pint chicken stock	⅔ cup chicken stock
bay leaf	bay leaf
blade mace	blade mace
few peppercorns	few peppercorns
salt and freshly ground black pepper	salt and freshly ground black pepper
slice lemon	slice lemon
few drops lemon juice	few drops lemon juice
15 g/½ oz butter	1 tablespoon butter
15 g/½ oz flour	2 tablespoons all-purpose flour
Garnish:	Garnish:
few white grapes	few green grapes
watercress	watercress
croûtons	croûtons

Roll the plaice fillets and secure with a wooden cocktail stick if necessary. Place the fish in the shallow dish and pour over the wine, stock, bay leaf, blade mace, few peppercorns, salt and pepper, lemon slice and juice. Cover with greaseproof paper and cook in the microwave for 5 minutes, turning the dish once during cooking. Carefully drain off the liquor and reserve. Keep the fish hot.

Mix the butter and flour together in the basin and pour the strained liquor over, whisking well. Cook in the microwave for 1 minute, stir and cook for a further minute. Pour over the plaice and garnish with grapes, watercress and croûtons.

Seafood curry

Utensil: 1.5-litre/2½-pint (U.S.
  3-pint) ovenproof soufflé dish
Microwave cooking time:
  11 minutes

Serves: 4

METRIC/IMPERIAL	AMERICAN
1 tablespoon oil	1 tablespoon oil
1 medium onion, chopped	1 medium onion, chopped
2 tablespoons curry powder	3 tablespoons curry powder
2 tablespoons flour	3 tablespoons all-purpose flour
300 ml/½ pint water	1¼ cups water
225 g/8 oz cod, skinned and cut into chunks	½ lb cod, skinned and cut into chunks
50 g/2 oz button mushrooms, sliced	½ cup sliced mushrooms
salt and freshly ground black pepper	salt and freshly ground black pepper
150 ml/¼ pint soured cream	⅔ cup sour cream
225 g/8 oz peeled prawns	½ lb peeled prawns or shrimp

Heat the oil in the soufflé dish in the microwave for 2 minutes. Add the onion and curry powder, stir well and cook in the microwave for 4 minutes. Add the flour and carefully stir in the water. Add the cod and mushrooms, mix well and season lightly. Cook for a further 4 minutes in the microwave, stirring every minute. Stir in the soured cream and prawns and heat in the microwave for 1 minute before serving with boiled rice.

Savoury fish crumble

Utensil: 1.75-litre/3-pint (U.S. 4-pint) round casserole dish
Microwave cooking time:
  13 minutes

Serves: 4

METRIC/IMPERIAL	AMERICAN
50 g/2 oz butter	¼ cup butter
1 medium onion, chopped	1 medium onion, chopped
1 tablespoon chopped green pepper	1 tablespoon chopped green pepper
450 g/1 lb cod fillet, skinned and boned	1 lb cod fillet, skinned and boned
salt and freshly ground black pepper	salt and freshly ground black pepper
75 g/3 oz fresh brown breadcrumbs	1½ cups fresh soft brown bread crumbs
grated rind of 1 lemon	grated rind of 1 lemon
50 g/2 oz red Leicester cheese, grated	½ cup grated cheese
2 tablespoons chopped parsley	3 tablespoons chopped parsley

Place the butter in the casserole dish and melt in the microwave for 1 minute. Add the onion and green pepper and cook in the microwave for 4 minutes, stirring twice. Add the flaked fish and season lightly. Cook in the microwave for a further 4 minutes, stirring every minute.

Mix together the remaining ingredients and cover the fish with the mixture. Heat in the microwave for 4 minutes, turning the dish twice.

Baked cod with orange and walnut topping

Utensil: 1.5-litre/2½-pint (U.S. 3-pint) shallow oblong casserole dish
Microwave cooking time: 10 minutes

Serves: 4

METRIC/IMPERIAL
25 g/1 oz butter
50 g/2 oz onion, chopped
450 g/1 lb cod fillet, skinned
salt and freshly ground black pepper
juice and grated rind of 1 orange
25 g/1 oz fresh brown breadcrumbs
50 g/2 oz walnuts, roughly chopped
Garnish:
orange segments
bunch watercress

AMERICAN
2 tablespoons butter
½ cup chopped onion
1 lb cod fillet, skinned
salt and freshly ground black pepper
juice and grated rind of 1 orange
½ cup fresh soft brown bread crumbs
½ cup roughly chopped walnuts
Garnish:
orange segments
bunch watercress

Melt the butter in the casserole dish in the microwave for 1 minute. Add the onion and cook in the microwave for a further 3 minutes. Place the fish in the dish, season lightly and pour over the orange juice. Cook in the microwave for 4 minutes, turning the fish once.

Mix together the orange rind, breadcrumbs and walnuts. Season lightly and place on top of the fish. Heat in the microwave for 2 minutes. Garnish with orange segments and watercress before serving.

Cod provençal

Utensil: 1.5-litre/2½-pint (U.S. 3-pint) oval ovenproof pie dish
Microwave cooking time: 6 minutes

Serves: 4

METRIC/IMPERIAL
450 g/1 lb cod, cubed
1 tablespoon oil
1 medium onion, finely chopped
1 clove garlic, crushed
2 tomatoes, skinned and sliced
salt and freshly ground black pepper
pinch basil
4 tablespoons stuffed olives, sliced
150 ml/¼ pint double cream
Garnish:
chopped parsley

AMERICAN
1 lb cod, cubed
1 tablespoon oil
1 medium onion, finely chopped
1 clove garlic, crushed
2 tomatoes, skinned and sliced
salt and freshly ground black pepper
pinch basil
⅓ cup sliced stuffed olives
⅔ cup heavy cream
Garnish:
chopped parsley

Place the cod, oil, onion and garlic in the pie dish. Cover and cook in the microwave for 3 minutes, stirring twice during cooking. Stir in the tomatoes, seasoning, basil and olives, cover and cook in the microwave for a further 2 minutes. Pour over the cream and heat in the microwave for 1 minute. Sprinkle with chopped parsley and serve.

Devilled crab

Illustrated opposite

Utensil: 900-ml/1½-pint (U.S. 2-pint) ovenproof basin
Microwave cooking time:
4–5 minutes

Serves: 2

METRIC/IMPERIAL	AMERICAN
15 g/½ oz butter	1 tablespoon butter
1 small shallot, finely chopped	1 small shallot, finely chopped
150 g/5 oz crabmeat	5 oz crabmeat
1 tablespoon dry sherry	1 tablespoon dry sherry
2 tablespoons fresh breadcrumbs	3 tablespoons fresh soft bread crumbs
pinch cayenne pepper	pinch cayenne pepper
few drops Worcestershire sauce	few drops Worcestershire sauce
1 teaspoon Dijon mustard	1 teaspoon Dijon mustard
salt and freshly ground black pepper	salt and freshly ground black pepper
Topping:	Topping:
1 tablespoon fresh breadcrumbs	1 tablespoon fresh soft bread crumbs
1 tablespoon grated Parmesan cheese	1 tablespoon grated Parmesan cheese
1 tablespoon chopped parsley	1 tablespoon chopped parsley
Garnish:	Garnish:
lemon slices	lemon slices
watercress sprigs	watercress sprigs

Place the butter and shallot in the basin and cook in the microwave for 3 minutes. Stir in the remaining ingredients until well combined. Divide the mixture between 2 scallop shells. Mix the topping ingredients and sprinkle over the devilled crab. Return to the microwave and heat for 1–2 minutes, until hot. Garnish with lemon slices and watercress sprigs. Serve with hot crusty bread.

Fish and mussel casserole with cider

Utensils: cook-bag, 1.5-litre/2½-pint (U.S. 3-pint) oval ovenproof dish, 600-ml/1-pint (U.S. 2½-cup) glass measuring jug
Microwave cooking time:
11–12 minutes

Serves: 4

METRIC/IMPERIAL	AMERICAN
1 tablespoon oil	1 tablespoon oil
1 onion, finely chopped	1 onion, finely chopped
½ red pepper, finely sliced	½ red pepper, finely sliced
1 small aubergine, finely sliced	1 small eggplant, finely sliced
few drops lemon juice	few drops lemon juice
450 g/1 lb cod or haddock, cut into bite-size pieces	1 lb cod or haddock, cut into bite-size pieces
1 (150-g/5¼-oz) can mussels, drained	1 (5¼-oz) can mussels, drained
300 ml/½ pint dry cider	1¼ cups cider
salt and freshly ground black pepper	salt and freshly ground black pepper
1 teaspoon fresh marjoram	1 teaspoon fresh marjoram
2 tablespoons chopped parsley	3 tablespoons chopped parsley
25 g/1 oz butter	2 tablespoons butter
25 g/1 oz flour	¼ cup all-purpose flour
Garnish:	Garnish:
lemon slices	lemon slices
watercress	watercress

Place the oil, onion, pepper and aubergine in the cook-bag, secure loosely with an elastic band and cook in the microwave for 4 minutes, rearranging the vegetables half way through the cooking time. Carefully transfer to the oval dish and add the lemon juice, fish, mussels, cider, seasoning and herbs. Cover with cling film and cook in the microwave for 5 minutes, stirring once.

Allow to stand for 2 minutes. Place the butter and flour in the measuring jug and mix well together. Strain the fish liquor into the jug, stirring well. Cook in the microwave for 2–3 minutes until thickened. Pour over the fish and reheat in the microwave if necessary. Garnish with lemon slices and watercress.

Stuffed herrings

Utensils: 1-litre/2-pint (U.S.
2½-pint) ovenproof pudding
basin, 1-litre/2-pint (U.S. 2½-
pint) shallow pie dish
Microwave cooking time:
10 minutes

Serves: 4

METRIC/IMPERIAL	AMERICAN
25 g/1 oz butter	2 tablespoons butter
50 g/2 oz onion, finely chopped	½ cup finely chopped onion
100 g/4 oz cooking apple, chopped	1 cup chopped baking apple
juice of ½ lemon	juice of ½ lemon
½ teaspoon dry mustard	½ teaspoon dry mustard
50 g/2 oz fresh white breadcrumbs	1 cup fresh soft white bread crumbs
½ teaspoon dried rosemary	½ teaspoon dried rosemary
salt and freshly ground black pepper	salt and freshly ground black pepper
4 herrings, cleaned and boned	4 herrings, cleaned and boned
Garnish:	Garnish:
lemon slices	lemon slices

Melt the butter in the pudding basin in the microwave for 1 minute then add the onion and cook in the microwave for 3 minutes. Toss the apple in the lemon juice and add to the onion and butter together with the mustard, breadcrumbs and rosemary. Season lightly.

Divide the stuffing between the herrings and wrap them separately in greaseproof paper. Place 2 herrings in the pie dish and cook in the microwave for 3 minutes. Repeat with the second pair of herrings.

Carefully remove the greaseproof paper and place the herrings in a serving dish. Garnish with lemon slices.

Herrings in herby cream sauce

Utensils: 1-litre/2-pint (U.S. 2½-
pint) round shallow ovenproof
pie dish, 600-ml/1-pint (U.S. 2½-
cup) glass measuring jug
Microwave cooking time:
11 minutes 15 seconds

Serves: 4

METRIC/IMPERIAL	AMERICAN
salt and freshly ground black pepper	salt and freshly ground black pepper
8 herring fillets	8 herring fillets
50 g/2 oz onion, chopped	½ cup chopped onion
juice of ½ lemon	juice of ½ lemon
1 tablespoon chopped mixed fresh basil, thyme and parsley	1 tablespoon chopped mixed fresh basil, thyme and parsley
150 ml/¼ pint fish stock	⅔ cup fish stock
150 ml/¼ pint double cream	⅔ cup heavy cream
2 teaspoons cornflour	2 teaspoons cornstarch
1 tablespoon water	1 tablespoon water

Season the fish and roll up, with skin outside, from head to tail. Secure with wooden cocktail sticks and place 4 at a time in the pie dish. Cook in the microwave for 3 minutes. Repeat with the other 4 fillets.

Place the onion and lemon juice in the measuring jug, season lightly and cook in the microwave for 3 minutes. Add the herbs, stock and cream. Heat in the microwave for 2 minutes. Blend the cornflour with the water and stir into the sauce. Thicken in the microwave for 15 seconds, stir well and pour a little over the fish. Serve the remaining sauce separately.

Haddock mornay

Utensil: 1-litre/1½-pint (U.S. 2-pint) oblong ovenproof dish
Microwave cooking time:
    4–5 minutes

Serves: 4

METRIC/IMPERIAL
350 g/12 oz haddock
2 tablespoons milk
15 g/½ oz butter
2 eggs, hard-boiled and chopped
3 tomatoes, skinned and sliced
300 ml/½ pint parsley sauce (see page 78)
salt and freshly ground black pepper
50 g/2 oz cheese, grated
25 g/1 oz fresh breadcrumbs
Garnish:
stuffed olives
watercress

AMERICAN
12 oz haddock
3 tablespoons milk
1 tablespoon butter
2 eggs, hard-cooked and chopped
3 tomatoes, skinned and sliced
1¼ cups parsley sauce (see page 78)
salt and freshly ground black pepper
½ cup grated cheese
½ cup fresh soft bread crumbs
Garnish:
stuffed olives
watercress

Place the haddock, milk and butter in the dish and cook in the microwave for 3 minutes. Remove the fish and flake. Return to the dish with the hard-boiled eggs, tomatoes, parsley sauce and seasoning. Mix well and sprinkle with the cheese and breadcrumbs. Heat in the microwave for 1–2 minutes or until the cheese has melted. Garnish with the olives and watercress.
Note: If preferred the final cooking of the cheese and breadcrumbs can be done under a preheated grill.

Haddock in creamy cider sauce

Utensil: 2.25-litre/4-pint (U.S. 5-pint) deep oblong casserole dish
Microwave cooking time:
    11 minutes

Serves: 4

METRIC/IMPERIAL
450 g/1 lb haddock fillet, skinned
50 g/2 oz onion, chopped
50 g/2 oz button mushrooms, sliced
salt and freshly ground black pepper
300 ml/½ pint dry cider
3 teaspoons cornflour
2 teaspoons water
4 tablespoons double cream

AMERICAN
1 lb haddock fillet, skinned
½ cup chopped onion
½ cup sliced mushrooms
salt and freshly ground black pepper
1¼ cups cider
2 teaspoons cornstarch
2 teaspoons water
⅓ cup heavy cream

Place the haddock in the casserole dish together with the onion and mushrooms. Season lightly, pour over the cider and cook in the microwave for 5 minutes, turning the fish once.

Remove the fish from the dish and keep warm. Return the sauce to the oven and cook in the microwave for a further 5 minutes, stirring twice.

Blend the cornflour with the water and add to the sauce; thicken in the microwave for 1 minute, stirring once. Stir the double cream into the sauce, taste and adjust seasoning if necessary before pouring over the fish.

Peppered steaks with Madeira (page 41) in preparation and the finished dish

Salmon quiche

Utensils: 1.75-litre/3-pint (U.S. 4-pint) ovenproof pudding basin, 18-cm/7-inch ovenproof quiche dish, 1-litre/2-pint (U.S. 2½-pint) ovenproof soufflé dish
Microwave cooking time:
  8–10 minutes

Serves: 4

METRIC/IMPERIAL	AMERICAN
100 g/4 oz plain savoury biscuits	¼ lb crackers
100 g/4 oz butter	½ cup butter
50 g/2 oz cheese, finely grated	½ cup finely grated cheese
Filling:	Filling:
25 g/ 1 oz butter	2 tablespoons butter
50 g/2 oz onion, finely chopped	½ cup finely chopped onion
1 tablespoon flour	1 tablespoon all-purpose flour
1 (212-g/7½-oz) can red salmon	1 (7½-oz) can red salmon
3 tablespoons milk	¼ cup milk
grated rind of ½ lemon	grated rind of ½ lemon
1 tablespoon chopped parsley	1 tablespoon chopped parsley
Garnish:	Garnish:
tomato slices	tomato slices
watercress sprigs	watercress sprigs

Place the biscuits in a polythene bag and crush with a rolling pin. Melt the butter in the pudding basin in the microwave for 2 minutes, then stir in the biscuits and grated cheese. Press this mixture into the base and sides of the quiche dish, chill thoroughly.

Melt the butter for the filling in the soufflé dish in the microwave for 1 minute. Add the onion and cook in the microwave for 2 minutes. Stir in the flour then carefully add the liquid from the can of salmon, milk, lemon rind and parsley. Cook in the microwave for a further 3 minutes, stirring once during cooking. Stir in the flaked salmon, mix well and fill the prepared quiche dish. Smooth the top and garnish with slices of tomato and sprigs of watercress.

Serve chilled or reheat for 2 minutes in the microwave oven, turning the dish 4 times.
Note: This quiche is best served chilled as the crunchy case provides an excellent texture variation.

Trout in white wine

Utensils: 2 cook-bags, 600-ml/ 1-pint (U.S. 2½-cup) ovenproof pudding basin
Microwave cooking time:
  6½ minutes

Serves: 4

METRIC/IMPERIAL	AMERICAN
salt and freshly ground black pepper	salt and freshly ground black pepper
4 trout, cleaned and boned	4 trout, cleaned and boned
25 g/1 oz butter, melted	2 tablespoons melted butter
1 tablespoon chopped parsley	1 tablespoon chopped parsley
grated rind of 1 lemon	grated rind of 1 lemon
150 ml/¼ pint dry white wine	⅔ cup dry white wine
1 teaspoon cornflour	1 teaspoon cornstarch

Season the inside of the trout and brush with melted butter. Sprinkle the parsley and lemon rind inside the trout.

Place 2 fish in the cook-bag with the wine and secure loosely with an elastic band. Cook in the microwave for 3 minutes. Carefully split the bag and remove the fish to a serving dish.

Transfer the liquid to another cook-bag and cook the remaining trout in this in the microwave for 3 minutes. Reserve the cooking liquid and place in the pudding basin. Blend the cornflour with a little of the liquid then stir into the rest of the liquid and thicken in the microwave for 30 seconds. Pour over the trout before serving.

Meat, poultry and game

The microwave really comes into its own in this chapter. Joints of meat are literally cooked in minutes, for example a 1.25 kg/2¾ lb (U.S. 2¾ lb) piece of beef topside can be cooked in a total of 15 minutes!

A chart giving the cooking times and defrosting times for various meats can be found on page 60. Frozen meat can be successfully defrosted in the microwave in minutes, saving endless hours normally spent defrosting meat.

When making casseroles, use good quality meat as the rapid cooking of the microwave is not suitable for those cuts that require long slow cooking. Remember also that small pieces of meat cook more quickly than large pieces. If your microwave oven does not have a browning element and you want to brown chops, poultry or game for example, use a microwave browning dish (see page 9) or brown under a conventional grill.

Peppered steaks with Madeira

Illustrated on pages 38–39

Utensils: 1.5-litre/2½-pint (U.S. 3-pint) oblong shallow ovenproof dish, cook-bag
Microwave cooking time:
16 minutes

Serves: 4

METRIC/IMPERIAL	AMERICAN
50 g/2 oz butter	¼ cup butter
1 clove garlic, crushed	1 clove garlic, crushed
2 large onions, sliced	2 large onions, sliced
1 green pepper, sliced	1 green pepper, sliced
1 red pepper, sliced	1 red pepper, sliced
5 tablespoons Madeira	6 tablespoons Madeira
salt	salt
2 teaspoons Marmite	2 teaspoons yeast extract
4 (175-g/6-oz) rump steaks	4 (6-oz) rump steaks
20 black peppercorns, crushed	20 black peppercorns, crushed
Garnish:	Garnish:
watercress	watercress

Melt the butter in the oblong dish in the microwave for 2 minutes. Add the garlic, onions, green and red pepper. Toss well then place the dish in the cook-bag (or cover the dish with the bag split) and cook in the microwave for 5 minutes. Stir the vegetables and add 4 tablespoons of the Madeira. Season lightly with salt and replace the dish in the cook-bag. Continue to cook in the microwave for 5 minutes.

Mix the Marmite with the remaining Madeira and brush each side of the steaks with this mixture. Place them on the bed of vegetables and sprinkle the crushed peppercorns over the top. Return to the microwave and cook for 4 minutes, turning and rearranging the steaks once during cooking. (If the steaks are not cooked enough after 4 minutes for your liking, cook for a little longer.) Garnish with watercress.

Hungarian beef

Illustrated opposite

Utensil: 2.25-litre/4-pint (U.S. 5-pint) oblong deep ovenproof dish
Microwave cooking time: 21 minutes

Serves: 4

METRIC/IMPERIAL
25 g/1 oz butter
1 large onion, sliced
2 tablespoons flour
1 (134-g/4¾-oz) jar tomato purée
300 ml/½ pint brown stock
1 tablespoon paprika pepper
450 g/1 lb topside, cubed
225 g/8 oz tomatoes, skinned and
  chopped
salt and freshly ground black pepper

AMERICAN
2 tablespoons butter
1 large onion, sliced
3 tablespoons all-purpose flour
1 (4¾-oz) jar tomato paste
1¼ cups brown stock
1 tablespoon paprika pepper
1 lb top round, cubed
½ lb tomatoes, skinned and
  chopped
salt and freshly ground black pepper

Melt the butter in the casserole dish in the microwave for 1 minute. Add the onion and cook in the microwave for a further 5 minutes. Stir in the flour and gradually add the tomato purée, stock and paprika pepper. Add the meat, stir well and cook in the microwave for 15 minutes, stirring every 2 minutes.

Stir in the tomatoes, cover with foil and leave to stand for 3–5 minutes. Adjust the seasoning before serving. Serve from the dish or transfer to a heated serving dish.

Herby meatballs

Illustrated on page 99

Utensils: 1.5-litre/2½-pint (U.S. 3-pint) shallow oval ovenproof dish
Microwave cooking time: 15 minutes

Serves: 4

METRIC/IMPERIAL
450 g/1 lb minced beef
1 medium onion, grated
6 tablespoons fresh white or brown
  breadcrumbs
½ teaspoon mixed dried herbs
salt and freshly ground black pepper
1 egg, beaten
50 g/2 oz butter
2 tablespoons flour
150 ml/¼ pint red wine
2 tablespoons tomato purée
1 beef stock cube, crumbled
300 ml/½ pint boiling water
Garnish:
chopped spring onions

AMERICAN
1 lb ground beef
1 medium onion, grated
7 tablespoons fresh soft white or
  brown bread crumbs
½ teaspoon mixed dried herbs
salt and freshly ground black pepper
1 egg, beaten
¼ cup butter
3 tablespoons all-purpose flour
⅔ cup red wine
3 tablespoons tomato paste
1 beef bouillon cube, crumbled
1¼ cups boiling water
Garnish:
chopped scallions

Mix together the beef, onion, breadcrumbs and herbs. Season lightly and bind with the beaten egg. Shape into 16 meatballs, each about the size of a walnut.

Place the butter in the oval dish and melt in the microwave for 2 minutes. Toss the meatballs in the butter and return to the microwave for 5 minutes, turning the meatballs once during cooking. Add the flour to absorb the butter and gradually stir in the remaining ingredients. Cook in the microwave for 8 minutes, turning the meatballs 3 times during cooking. Garnish with the chopped spring onions before serving.

Chilli con carne

Utensil: 2.25-litre/4-pint (U.S. 5-pint) oblong casserole dish
Microwave cooking time:
    33 minutes

Serves: 4

METRIC/IMPERIAL	AMERICAN
1 onion, finely chopped	1 onion, finely chopped
1 small green pepper, finely chopped	1 small green pepper, finely chopped
2 carrots, diced	2 carrots, diced
1 tablespoon oil	1 tablespoon oil
350 g/12 oz minced beef	1½ cups ground beef
150 ml/¼ pint tomato juice	⅔ cup tomato juice
150 ml/¼ pint beef stock	⅔ cup beef stock
1 (227-g/8-oz) can tomatoes	1 (8-oz) can tomatoes
½–1 tablespoon chilli powder, according to taste	½–1 tablespoon chili powder, according to taste
salt and freshly ground black pepper	salt and freshly ground black pepper
1 (280-g/10-oz) can kidney beans, drained	1 (10-oz) can kidney beans, drained
Garnish:	Garnish:
2 tablespoons chopped parsley	3 tablespoons chopped parsley

Place the onion, pepper, carrots and oil in the casserole dish and cook in the microwave for 5 minutes, stirring once. Add the meat and continue to cook in the microwave for 4 minutes. Add all the remaining ingredients, except for the kidney beans, cover and continue to cook for 22 minutes, stirring twice during cooking. Stir in the kidney beans and reheat for 2 minutes. Garnish with chopped parsley.

Meatloaf with pepper sauce

Utensils: 2.25-litre/4-pint (U.S. 5-pint) ovenproof mixing bowl, 1-litre/1½-pint (U.S. 2-pint) oblong ovenproof pie dish, 600-ml/1-pint (U.S. 2½-cup) glass measuring jug
Microwave cooking time:
    19 minutes

Serves: 4

METRIC/IMPERIAL	AMERICAN
1 tablespoon oil	1 tablespoon oil
1 large onion, chopped	1 large onion, chopped
225 g/8 oz minced beef	1 cup ground beef
225 g/8 oz minced pork	1 cup ground pork
6 tablespoons fresh brown bread-crumbs	7 tablespoons fresh soft brown bread crumbs
1 clove garlic, crushed	1 clove garlic, crushed
1 tablespoon tomato purée	1 tablespoon tomato paste
salt and freshly ground black pepper	salt and freshly ground black pepper
1 egg, beaten	1 egg, beaten
Sauce:	Sauce:
25 g/1 oz butter	2 tablespoons butter
100 g/4 oz green pepper, chopped	1 cup chopped green pepper
1 tablespoon flour	1 tablespoon all-purpose flour
300 ml/½ pint boiling water	1¼ cups boiling water
1 beef stock cube	1 beef bouillon cube
1 tablespoon tomato purée	1 tablespoon tomato paste
50 g/2 oz button mushrooms, sliced	½ cup sliced button mushrooms
Garnish:	Garnish:
tomato wedges	tomato wedges
watercress	watercress

Place the oil in the mixing bowl and heat in the microwave for 2 minutes. Add the onion and cook for 3 minutes, stirring once. Stir in the meats, breadcrumbs, garlic and tomato purée; season with salt and black pepper then bind with the beaten egg. Mix well and press into the pie dish. Cook in the microwave for 5 minutes, turning the dish twice during cooking. Wrap completely in foil, placing the shiny side of the foil inwards, leave to rest for 15 minutes. Remove the foil and return to the microwave for a further 3 minutes then wrap in foil, as before, and rest for 5 minutes.

Place the butter for the sauce in the measuring jug, and melt in the microwave for 1 minute. Add the green pepper and stir well; return to the microwave for 3 minutes. Stir in the flour and carefully add the water and crumbled stock cube, tomato purée and mushrooms. Cook in the microwave for 2 minutes, stirring once. Taste and season the sauce. Turn out the meatloaf and serve with some of the sauce poured over. Garnish with tomato wedges and watercress. Serve the remaining sauce in a jug or sauceboat.

Steak and kidney pie

Utensil: 1.5-litre/2½-pint (U.S. 3-pint) oval ovenproof pie dish
Microwave cooking time:
    40 minutes plus conventional oven time 20–30 minutes

Serves: 4

METRIC/IMPERIAL	AMERICAN
1 onion, thinly sliced	1 onion, thinly sliced
25 g/1 oz butter	2 tablespoons butter
1 tablespoon oil	1 tablespoon oil
450 g 1 lb chuck steak, cubed	1 lb chuck steak, cubed
100 g/4 oz ox kidney, sliced	¼ lb beef kidney, sliced
seasoned flour	seasoned flour
150 ml/¼ pint red wine	⅔ cup red wine
300 ml/½ pint beef stock	1¼ cups beef stock
1 tablespoon Worcestershire sauce	1 tablespoon Worcestershire sauce
1 bay leaf	1 bay leaf
mace	mace
salt and freshly ground black pepper	salt and freshly ground black pepper
100 g/4 oz button mushrooms	1 cup button mushrooms
1 (198-g/7-oz) packet frozen puff pastry	1 (7-oz) package frozen puff paste
1 egg, beaten	1 egg, beaten

Place the onion, butter and oil in the pie dish and cook in the microwave for 4 minutes, stirring once during cooking. Toss the meat and kidney in seasoned flour and add to the onions. Cook in the microwave for 3 minutes. Add all the remaining ingredients except the mushrooms. Cover and cook in the microwave for 20 minutes, stirring frequently. Stand for 5 minutes. Cook in the microwave for a further 13 minutes. Stir in the mushrooms. Allow the meat to cool in the dish before covering with pastry.

To finish the pie, roll out the pastry to an oval shape on a lightly floured board. Cut off a thin border of pastry from the edge and line the rim of the pie dish. Dampen the edges and cover with the pastry. Seal the edges and flute. Make a hole in the centre and brush with beaten egg. Bake in a hot conventional oven (220°C, 425°F, Gas Mark 7) for 20–30 minutes.

Beef olives

Illustrated opposite

Utensil: 2.25-litre/4-pint (U.S. 5-
   pint) deep oblong casserole dish
Microwave cooking time:
   21 minutes

Serves: 4

METRIC/IMPERIAL
25 g/1 oz dry white breadcrumbs
50 g/2 oz mushrooms, finely chopped
½ teaspoon dried mixed herbs
1 tablespoon lemon juice
3 tablespoons milk
salt and freshly ground black pepper
450 g/1 lb topside, thinly sliced
25 g/1 oz butter
225 g/8 oz small onions
2 tablespoons flour
450 ml/¾ pint good brown stock
2 tablespoons dry sherry
100 g/4 oz small button mushrooms
225 g/8 oz long grain rice, cooked
   (see page 93)
Garnish:
chopped parsley

AMERICAN
¼ cup fine dry white bread crumbs
½ cup finely chopped mushrooms
½ teaspoon dried mixed herbs
1 tablespoon lemon juice
¼ cup milk
salt and freshly ground black pepper
1 lb top round, thinly sliced
2 tablespoons butter
½ lb small onions
3 tablespoons all-purpose flour
2 cups good brown stock
3 tablespoons dry sherry
1 cup small button mushrooms
1 cup long grain rice, cooked
   (see page 93)
Garnish:
chopped parsley

Mix together the breadcrumbs, chopped mushrooms, herbs, lemon juice and milk. Season and divide this stuffing between the slices of topside. Roll up the meat, folding in the sides to form neat parcels and secure with string.

Place the butter in the casserole dish and melt in the microwave for 1 minute, then add the onions and cook for a further 5 minutes. Stir in the flour and carefully add the stock, sherry and mushrooms. Stir well.

Place the meat in the dish with the sauce and cook in the microwave for 15 minutes, turning the meat over and round every 2 minutes. Leave to stand for 3 minutes before transferring to a serving dish.

Serve on a bed of hot rice and arrange the mushrooms and onions from the sauce on top of the beef olives; string removed. Garnish with a little chopped parsley before serving.

Boeuf à la bourguignonne

Utensil: 1.5-litre/2½-pint (U.S. 3-
   pint) oval ovenproof pie dish
Microwave cooking time:
   41 minutes

Serves: 4

METRIC/IMPERIAL
4 rashers bacon, cut into strips
1 onion, chopped
450 g/1 lb chuck steak, cubed
300 ml/½ pint beef stock
150 ml/¼ pint red wine
1 clove garlic, crushed
bouquet garni
salt and freshly ground black pepper
8 button onions, peeled and left whole
100 g/4 oz button mushrooms
Garnish:
2 tablespoons chopped parsley

AMERICAN
4 bacon slices, cut into strips
1 onion, chopped
1 lb chuck steak, cubed
1¼ cups beef stock
⅔ cup red wine
1 clove garlic, crushed
bouquet garni
salt and freshly ground black pepper
8 button onions, peeled and left whole
1 cup button mushrooms
Garnish:
3 tablespoons chopped parsley

Place the bacon and onion in the pie dish and cook in the microwave for 4 minutes, stirring every minute. Add the meat and cook in the microwave for 2 minutes. Stir in the stock, red wine, garlic, bouquet garni, seasoning and button onions and cook in the microwave for 30 minutes, stirring 3 times during cooking. Add the mushrooms and cook for a further 5 minutes. Allow to stand for 5 minutes before serving.

Garnish with chopped parsley.

Tipsy kidneys

Illustrated on page 95

Utensils: 1.5-litre/2½-pint (U.S. 3-pint) oval ovenproof pie dish, 1.5-litre/2½-pint (U.S. 3-pint) ovenproof pudding basin
Microwave cooking time: 27–28 minutes

Serves: 4

METRIC/IMPERIAL	AMERICAN
1 onion, finely chopped	1 onion, finely chopped
15 g/½ oz butter	1 tablespoon butter
1 tablespoon oil	1 tablespoon oil
10 lambs' kidneys, skinned, cored and halved	10 lamb kidneys, skinned, cored and halved
1 tablespoon flour	1 tablespoon all-purpose flour
salt and freshly ground black pepper	salt and freshly ground black pepper
2 tablespoons tomato purée	3 tablespoons tomato paste
300 ml/½ pint chicken stock, made with a stock cube	1¼ cups chicken stock, made with a bouillon cube
4 frankfurters, sliced	4 frankfurters, sliced
100 g/4 oz button mushrooms	1 cup button mushrooms
3 tablespoons whisky or sherry	¼ cup whiskey or sherry
450 ml/¾ pint hand hot water (about 48°C/120°F)	2 cups hand hot water (about 120°F)
225 g/8 oz long grain rice	1 cup long grain rice
½ teaspoon salt	½ teaspoon salt
Garnish:	Garnish:
chopped parsley	chopped parsley

Place the onion, butter and oil in the oval dish and cook in the microwave for 4 minutes, stirring once. Stir in the kidneys and return to the microwave for 5 minutes, stirring once during cooking. Add the flour and mix well, then add all the remaining ingredients, except the whisky or sherry, water, rice and salt. Cook in the microwave for 8 minutes. Stir in the whisky or sherry and allow to stand while cooking the rice.

Place the water, rice and salt in the pudding basin and cook in the microwave for 10–11 minutes. Stir well, arrange a border round the edge of a warmed serving dish and place the kidneys in centre. Garnish with chopped parsley.

Mexican liver

Utensil: 2.25-litre/4-pint (U.S. 5-pint) deep oblong ovenproof dish
Microwave cooking time: 12 minutes

Serves: 4

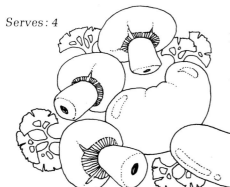

METRIC/IMPERIAL	AMERICAN
2 tablespoons oil	3 tablespoons oil
1 onion, sliced	1 onion, sliced
1 (100-g/4-oz) green pepper, sliced	1 (4-oz) green pepper, sliced
1 clove garlic, crushed	1 clove garlic, crushed
225 g/8 oz lamb's liver, sliced	½ lb lamb liver, sliced
100 g/4 oz button mushrooms	1 cup button mushrooms
1 (397-g/14-oz) can tomatoes	1 (14-oz) can tomatoes
3 tablespoons water	¼ cup water
salt and freshly ground black pepper	salt and freshly ground black pepper

Heat the oil in the dish in the microwave for 2 minutes. Add the onion, green pepper and garlic and cook in the microwave for 4 minutes, stirring once during cooking. Add the liver and cook in the microwave for a further minute before mixing in the remaining ingredients. Season and continue to cook in the microwave for a final 5 minutes, stirring once during cooking. Leave to stand for a few minutes before serving.

Somerset gammon steaks

Utensil: 2.25-litre/4-pint (U.S. 5-pint) deep oblong casserole dish
Microwave cooking time:
   19 minutes

Serves: 4

METRIC/IMPERIAL	AMERICAN
4 gammon steaks	4 cured ham slices
50 g/2 oz onion, thinly sliced	2 oz onion, thinly sliced
300 ml/½ pint apple juice	1¼ cups apple juice
1 heaped teaspoon cornflour	1 heaped teaspoon cornstarch
1 large eating apple	1 large eating apple
juice of ½ lemon	juice of ½ lemon
Garnish:	Garnish:
watercress sprigs	watercress sprigs

Place the gammon steaks in the casserole dish and cook in the microwave for 6 minutes, turning the steaks over and round once. Add the onion rings, re-arrange the gammon and return to the microwave for a further 4 minutes.

Remove the gammon from the dish and add the apple juice to the onion. Cook in the microwave for 5 minutes. Blend the cornflour with a little of the cooking liquid then stir back into the dish. Continue to cook in the microwave for 2 minutes, stirring twice during cooking.

Core the apple and cut into rings, leaving the skin on to provide colour. Dip each apple ring in lemon juice to prevent discoloration and garnish each gammon steak with an apple ring. Pour the sauce into a sauceboat and reheat the gammon steaks in the casserole dish for 2 minutes.

Transfer to a serving plate, garnish with watercress and serve with the sauce.

Somerset pork with cider cream sauce

Illustrated on page 79

Utensil: 2.25-litre/4-pint (U.S. 5-pint) oval casserole dish
Microwave cooking time:
   26 minutes

Serves: 4

METRIC/IMPERIAL	AMERICAN
25 g/1 oz butter	2 tablespoons butter
225 g/8 oz onions, chopped	2 cups chopped onion
0.75 kg/1½ lb pork fillet, trimmed and cubed	1½ lb pork tenderloin, trimmed and cubed
100 g/4 oz button mushrooms, sliced	1 cup sliced button mushrooms
300 ml/½ pint dry cider	1¼ cups cider
salt and freshly ground black pepper	salt and freshly ground black pepper
2 tablespoons cornflour	3 tablespoons cornstarch
1 tablespoon water	1 tablespoon water
2 tablespoons double cream	3 tablespoons heavy cream
Garnish:	Garnish:
chopped parsley	chopped parsley

Place the butter in the casserole dish and melt in the microwave for 1 minute. Add the onion and cook for a further 5 minutes. Stir in the cubed pork and cook in the microwave for 8 minutes, stirring 4 times. Add the mushrooms and cider and season lightly. Cook in the microwave for 10 minutes, stirring 4 times. Blend the cornflour with the water and stir into the casserole then return to the microwave for a further 2 minutes.

Stir the double cream into the sauce and garnish with parsley.
Note: If you prefer the meat to be browner, seal the pork under a preheated grill before cooking in the microwave. The timing will be slightly reduced if this method is chosen.

Prune and almond stuffed pork

Illustrated opposite

Utensils: 1-litre/2-pint (U.S. 2½-pint) ovenproof pudding basin, 2.25-litre/4-pint (U.S. 5-pint) oblong ovenproof dish or microwave browning dish
Microwave cooking time:
  41 minutes

Serves: 4–6

METRIC/IMPERIAL	AMERICAN
225 g/8 oz prunes, stoned and chopped	½ lb prunes, pitted and chopped
450 ml/¾ pint boiling chicken stock	2 cups boiling chicken stock
50 g/2 oz blanched whole almonds	½ cup blanched whole almonds
1.5 kg/3 lb boned and skinned belly and hand of pork	3 lb boned and skinned sirloin roast of pork
225 g/8 oz streaky bacon rashers	½ lb bacon slices
2 tablespoons clear honey	3 tablespoons clear honey

Mix the prunes and chicken stock together in the pudding basin and cook in the microwave for 20 minutes, stirring every 5 minutes, until all the water is absorbed. Mix in the blanched almonds.

Lay the pork flat on a clean surface, skinned side downwards. Slit the hand end of the joint with a sharp knife and open out flat. Spread the prune stuffing over the pork and carefully bring the two sides of the meat together, to enclose the stuffing and form a roll. Secure firmly with string. Brown under a pre-heated grill, if liked. Wrap the bacon around the pork and secure with wooden cocktail sticks. Place the meat in the oblong dish and cook in the microwave for 10 minutes, turning over twice. Allow to stand for 10 minutes then return to the microwave for a further 5 minutes. Again rest for 10 minutes and finally return to the microwave for 5 minutes.

Wrap in foil, with the shiny side inwards, and leave to stand for 20–30 minutes before serving. Remove from the foil and place on a serving dish.

Place the honey and 1 tablespoon of the pork drippings in the pudding basin and heat in the microwave for 1 minute. Brush the pork with this glaze before serving.
Note: If using the microwave browning dish, there is no need to brown the meat under the grill. Preheat the browning dish in the microwave with 1 tablespoon oil for 4 minutes before putting the meat in the dish (see page 9). Seal the meat on all sides and then continue to cook as above.

Pork casserole with apple

Illustrated on page 62

Utensil: 2.25-litre/4-pint (U.S. 5-pint) deep casserole dish
Microwave cooking time:
  20 minutes

Serves: 4

METRIC/IMPERIAL	AMERICAN
25 g/1 oz butter	2 tablespoons butter
1 large onion, quartered	1 large onion, quartered
1 tablespoon flour	1 tablespoon all-purpose flour
0.75 kg/1½ lb lean pork, cut in bite-size pieces	1½ lb lean pork, cut in bite-size pieces
few sprigs mixed fresh herbs, tied in a bundle	few sprigs mixed fresh herbs, tied in a bundle
175 ml/6 fl oz dry white wine	¾ cup dry white wine
salt and freshly ground black pepper	salt and freshly ground black pepper
1 large green-skinned eating apple, cored and sliced	1 large green-skinned eating apple, cored and sliced
juice of ½ lemon	juice of ½ lemon
50 g/2 oz mushrooms, sliced	½ cup sliced mushrooms

Cook the butter and onion in the casserole dish in the microwave for 8 minutes. Stir in the flour, add the meat and herbs and carefully stir in the wine. Season lightly and cook in the microwave for 7 minutes, stirring 3 times.

Dip the apple slices in the lemon juice to prevent discoloration and add to the casserole together with the mushrooms. Cook in the microwave for 5 minutes, stirring once during cooking. Remove the herbs from the casserole before serving.

Sweet 'n' sour lamb

Utensil: 1.5-litre/2½-pint (U.S. 3-
   pint) oval ovenproof pie dish
Microwave cooking time:
   27 minutes

Serves: 4

METRIC/IMPERIAL	AMERICAN
1 onion, finely chopped	1 onion, finely chopped
2 sticks celery, finely sliced	2 stalks celery, finely sliced
1 tablespoon oil	1 tablespoon oil
0.75 kg/1½ lb lean shoulder of lamb, cubed	1½ lb lean shoulder of lamb, cubed
seasoned flour	seasoned flour
1 (396-g/14-oz) can tomatoes	1 (14-oz) can tomatoes
2 tablespoons tomato purée	3 tablespoons tomato paste
2 tablespoons wine vinegar	3 tablespoons wine vinegar
1 tablespoons brown sugar	1 tablespoon brown sugar
300 ml/½ pint stock	1¼ cups stock
1 tablespoon redcurrant jelly	1 tablespoon red currant jelly
1 teaspoon dried basil	1 teaspoon dried basil
salt and freshly ground black pepper	salt and freshly ground black pepper

Place the onion, celery and oil in the pie dish and cook in the microwave for 5 minutes, stirring twice during cooking. Toss the meat in seasoned flour and add to the vegetables. Cook in the microwave for 2 minutes. Add the remaining ingredients, cover and continue to cook in the microwave for 20 minutes, stirring twice during cooking. Allow to stand for 10 minutes before serving.

Quick lamb chops

Illustrated on the jacket

Utensils: 1.5-litre/2½-pint (U.S. 3-
   pint) shallow oblong casserole
   dish, 23-cm/9-inch round ovenproof dinner plate, kitchen paper
Microwave cooking time:
   11 minutes

Serves: 3

METRIC/IMPERIAL	AMERICAN
75 g/3 oz softened butter	6 tablespoons softened butter
grated rind of 1 lemon	grated rind of 1 lemon
1 teaspoon lemon juice	1 teaspoon lemon juice
6 lamb chops	6 lamb chops
garlic salt	garlic salt
freshly ground black pepper	freshly ground black pepper
3 firm tomatoes	3 firm tomatoes
Garnish:	Garnish:
watercress	watercress

Beat the softened butter with the lemon rind and juice. Place the chops in the oblong dish and dot each with the lemon butter. Reserve a little butter for the tomatoes. Season with a little garlic salt and freshly ground black pepper then cook in the microwave for 10 minutes, turning the chops over and rearranging them 3 times during cooking.

   Place the tomatoes on the dinner plate and surround them by kitchen paper (this helps to support the tomatoes and prevent them from collapsing). Cut a cross in the top of each tomato and dot with the remaining lemon butter. Cook in the microwave for 1 minute, turning the plate once during cooking. Arrange the chops on a serving dish together with the tomatoes and garnish with watercress. If liked, serve with jacket potatoes cooked in the microwave oven (see page 73).

Lamb in onion and caraway sauce

Illustrated on page 90

Utensil: 2.25-litre/4-pint (U.S. 5-pint) deep round ovenproof dish
Microwave cooking time:
  20 minutes

Serves: 4

METRIC/IMPERIAL	AMERICAN
50 g/2 oz butter	¼ cup butter
100 g/4 oz onion, chopped	1 cup chopped onion
0.75 kg/1½ lb lean lamb (e.g. boned fillet from leg)	1½ lb lean lamb (e.g. boned tenderloin from leg)
2 tablespoons flour	3 tablespoons all-purpose flour
1 teaspoon tarragon vinegar	1 teaspoon tarragon vinegar
1 tablespoon caraway seeds	1 tablespoon caraway seeds
300 ml/½ pint boiling stock	1¼ cups boiling stock
salt and freshly ground black pepper	salt and freshly ground black pepper

Melt the butter in the dish in the microwave for 1 minute. Add the onion and cook in the microwave for 2 minutes. Cut the lamb into cubes, add to the onion and continue to cook in the microwave for 7 minutes, stirring twice.

Stir in the flour, tarragon vinegar and caraway seeds then carefully add the stock. Season lightly and thicken in the microwave for 10 minutes, stirring 4 times. Taste and adjust seasoning before serving with boiled rice.

Chicken and water chestnut pilaf

Utensils: 2.25-litre/4-pint (U.S. 5-pint) oblong casserole dish, 600-ml/1-pint (U.S. 2½-cup) glass measuring jug
Microwave cooking time:
  26 minutes

Serves: 4

METRIC/IMPERIAL	AMERICAN
1 onion, finely chopped	1 onion, finely chopped
15 g/½ oz butter	1 tablespoon butter
1 tablespoon oil	1 tablespoon oil
4 chicken breasts	4 chicken breasts
300 ml/½ pint apple juice	1¼ cups apple juice
¼ teaspoon turmeric	¼ teaspoon turmeric
salt and freshly ground black pepper	salt and freshly ground black pepper
1 (227-g/8-oz) can water chestnuts, drained and sliced	1 (8-oz) can water chestnuts, drained and sliced
10 stuffed olives, halved	10 stuffed olives, halved
1 tablespoon cornflour	1 tablespoon cornstarch
Pilaf rice:	Pilaf rice:
300 ml/½ pint hand hot water (about 48°C/120°F)	1¼ cups hand hot water (about 120°F)
100 g/4 oz long grain rice	½ cup long grain rice
¼ teaspoon turmeric	¼ teaspoon turmeric
Garnish:	Garnish:
chopped parsley	chopped parsley

Place the onion, butter and oil in the casserole and cook in the microwave for 5 minutes, stirring twice. Add the chicken to the dish and cook for 4 minutes, turning over after 2 minutes.

Stir in the apple juice, turmeric and seasoning, and cook in the microwave for 5 minutes. Add the water chestnuts and olives, continue to cook for a further 2 minutes. Blend the cornflour with a little water and stir into the chicken mixture. Cover and allow to stand whilst cooking the rice.

For the pilaf rice, place all the ingredients in the measuring jug and cook in the microwave for 10 minutes. Stir well and serve with the chicken piled on top. Garnish with chopped parsley.

Chicken with vegetables in wine

Illustrated opposite

Utensils: 600-ml/1-pint (U.S. 2½-cup) oval ovenproof pie dish, 1.75-litre/3-pint (U.S. 4-pint) oblong ovenproof dish, 1.5-litre/2½-pint (U.S. 3-pint) shallow oblong ovenproof dish
Microwave cooking time: 31 minutes

Serves: 4

METRIC/IMPERIAL
1 (1.5-kg/3¼-lb) chicken
25 g/1 oz butter
225 g/8 oz small onions, peeled
225 g/8 oz carrots, thickly sliced
100 g/4 oz streaky bacon, chopped
1 green pepper, deseeded and chopped
2 sticks celery, sliced
100 g/4 oz small button mushrooms
1 bay leaf
salt and freshly ground black pepper
2 tablespoons flour
300 ml/½ pint medium dry white wine
300 ml/½ pint chicken stock

AMERICAN
1 (3¼-lb) broiler/fryer chicken
2 tablespoons butter
½ lb small onions, peeled
½ lb carrots, thickly sliced
¼ lb bacon slices, chopped
1 green pepper, deseeded and chopped
2 stalks celery, sliced
1 cup small button mushrooms
1 bay leaf
salt and freshly ground black pepper
3 tablespoons all-purpose flour
1¼ cups medium dry white wine
1¼ cups chicken stock

Tie the legs of the chicken together firmly to hold them as close to the body of the bird as possible. Place the chicken on the upturned pie dish in the larger oblong dish. Cook in the microwave for 5 minutes, turning the dish round and the bird over at the end of the cooking time. Continue to cook in the microwave for a further 10 minutes, again turning the bird over 4 times and turning the dish round twice during the cooking time.

Wrap the chicken in a double thickness of foil with the shiny side inwards and allow to stand for 20–30 minutes before serving.

Melt the butter in the shallow dish in the microwave for 1 minute then add the onions, carrots, bacon, pepper and celery. Cook in the microwave for a further 5 minutes before adding the mushrooms and bay leaf. Season lightly and stir in the flour. Add the wine and stock and thicken in the microwave for 10 minutes, stirring twice.

Brown the chicken under a conventional grill, if liked, and then place in a serving dish. Arrange the vegetables in wine round the chicken.

Chicken tandoori

Utensil: 1-litre/2-pint (U.S. 2½-pint) shallow round ovenproof dish
Microwave cooking time: 20 minutes

Serves: 4

METRIC/IMPERIAL
4 chicken breasts
150 ml/¼ pint plain yogurt
grated rind of ½ lemon
1 tablespoon ground ginger
½ teaspoon turmeric
½ teaspoon garlic salt
salt and freshly ground black pepper

AMERICAN
4 chicken breasts
⅔ cup unflavored yogurt
grated rind of ½ lemon
1 tablespoon ground ginger
½ teaspoon turmeric
½ teaspoon garlic salt
salt and freshly ground black pepper

Slash the chicken at intervals, taking care only to penetrate halfway through the flesh. Mix the remaining ingredients together and spread over the chicken, pressing well in between the cuts. Cover with cling film and leave overnight.

Place in the shallow dish, cover with any remaining yogurt mixture and cook in the microwave for 5 minutes, turn the dish a quarter turn and continue to cook for a further 5 minutes. Alter the position of the chicken pieces and return to the microwave for 10 minutes, giving the dish a quarter turn after 5 minutes.

Chicken and artichoke casserole

Utensil: 2.25-litre/4-pint (U.S. 5-pint) oblong casserole dish
Microwave cooking time: 25 minutes

Serves: 4

METRIC/IMPERIAL	AMERICAN
4 chicken breasts	4 chicken breasts
25 g/1 oz flour	$\frac{1}{4}$ cup all-purpose flour
$\frac{1}{2}$ teaspoon paprika pepper	$\frac{1}{2}$ teaspoon paprika pepper
25 g/1 oz butter	2 tablespoons butter
1 small onion, finely chopped	1 small onion, finely chopped
150 ml/$\frac{1}{4}$ pint white wine	$\frac{2}{3}$ cup white wine
150 ml/$\frac{1}{4}$ pint chicken stock	$\frac{2}{3}$ cup chicken stock
grated rind of $\frac{1}{2}$ lemon	grated rind of $\frac{1}{2}$ lemon
salt and freshly ground black pepper	salt and freshly ground black pepper
1 tablespoon dried tarragon	1 tablespoon dried tarragon
1 (400-g/14-oz) can artichoke hearts	1 (14-oz) can artichoke hearts
150 ml/$\frac{1}{4}$ pint soured cream	$\frac{2}{3}$ cup sour cream

Skin the chicken and toss in the mixed flour and paprika pepper. Place the butter in the casserole and melt in the microwave for 1 minute. Add the floured chicken, cook in the microwave for 2 minutes, turn over and continue to cook for 3 minutes. Remove the chicken and stir in the onion. Return to the microwave for 5 minutes, stirring frequently. Add any remaining flour, the wine, stock, lemon rind, seasoning and tarragon. Return to the microwave for 4 minutes then replace the chicken in the casserole. Cover and cook in the microwave for 8 minutes. Stir in the drained artichokes and continue to cook in the microwave for 2 minutes. Lightly stir in the soured cream before serving.

Rolled galantine of chicken

Illustrated on page 11

Utensils: 2.25-litre/4-pint (U.S. 5-pint) oblong ovenproof dish, 1-litre/2-pint (U.S. 2$\frac{1}{2}$-pint) ovenproof soufflé dish, large oval shallow ovenproof meat dish (about 33 × 23 cm/13 × 9 inches)
Microwave cooking time: To defrost the chicken: 20 minutes. For the rolled galantine: 20 minutes

Serves: 4

METRIC/IMPERIAL	AMERICAN
1 frozen (1.5-kg/3$\frac{1}{2}$-lb) chicken, defrosted (see method) and boned	1 frozen (3$\frac{1}{2}$-lb) broiler/fryer chicken, defrosted (see method) and boned
100 g/4 oz onion, finely chopped	1 cup finely chopped onion
100 g/4 oz cooked ham, chopped	$\frac{1}{2}$ cup chopped cooked cured ham
100 g/4 oz cooked tongue, chopped	$\frac{1}{2}$ cup chopped cooked tongue
225 g/8 oz sausagemeat	1 cup sausage meat
1 tablespoon chopped fresh mixed herbs	1 tablespoon chopped fresh mixed herbs
2 tablespoons sherry	3 tablespoons sherry
2 tablespoons chopped black olives	3 tablespoons chopped ripe olives
1 tablespoons chopped stuffed olives	3 tablespoons chopped stuffed olives
salt and freshly ground black pepper	salt and freshly ground black pepper
Garnish:	Garnish:
tomato wedges	tomato wedges
watercress sprigs	watercress sprigs

Defrosting the chicken
To defrost the chicken, place the bird, breastside uppermost, in the oblong dish, having first opened the bag and removed any metal ties from the bird. Defrost in the microwave for 2 minutes and turn the chicken over, breastside down. Return to the microwave for 2 minutes more. Turn the bird over and rest for 5 minutes. Repeat this process 4 times more. Wrap the chicken in a double thickness of foil, placing the shiny side inwards to reflect the heat back into the bird. Leave to stand for 20 minutes then remove the giblets. Rinse the cavity with boiling water to ensure it is thoroughly defrosted.

Place the onion in the soufflé dish and cook in the microwave for 5 minutes. Add the ham, tongue and sausagemeat. Mix well then stir in the herbs, sherry and chopped olives; season lightly.

Bone the chicken and place, skin side down, on a board. Have ready a large needle threaded with double cotton — preferably in a colour easy to distinguish for removal. Spread the stuffing out over the chicken, splitting the legs down one side. Roll the chicken up from head to tail, tucking in any protruding flesh, to form a long thin sausage. Sew up firmly with the double cotton and place on the large oval meat dish. Cook in the microwave for 15 minutes, turning the dish round 3 times and turning the chicken over every 5 minutes. Remove any excess drippings with a baster during the cooking time. Remove the string from the chicken and wrap in foil, shiny side inwards, then allow to stand for 15 minutes before serving. Garnish with wedges of tomato and watercress before serving. This is also excellent served cold.
Note: The chicken was rolled from head to tail and not reshaped in the traditional way to produce a uniform shape which would cook particularly successfully in the microwave oven.

Pigeons in red wine

Illustrated on pages 58–59

Utensil: microwave browning dish
Microwave cooking time:
   28 minutes

Serves: 4

METRIC/IMPERIAL	AMERICAN
25 g/1 oz butter	2 tablespoons butter
1 tablespoon oil	1 tablespoon oil
2 pigeons, drawn and trussed	2 pigeons, drawn and trussed
4 rashers streaky bacon	4 bacon slices
1 onion, finely chopped	1 onion, finely chopped
1 tablespoon flour	1 tablespoon all-purpose flour
2 tablespoons redcurrant jelly	3 tablespoons red currant jelly
150 ml/$\frac{1}{4}$ pint red wine	$\frac{2}{3}$ cup red wine
150 ml/$\frac{1}{4}$ pint stock	$\frac{2}{3}$ cup stock
1 tablespoon tomato purée	1 tablespoon tomato paste
salt and freshly ground black pepper	salt and freshly ground black pepper
100 g/4 oz button mushrooms	1 cup button mushrooms
50 g/2 oz stuffed olives	$\frac{1}{3}$ cup stuffed olives
2 tablespoons chopped parsley	3 tablespoons chopped parsley
Garnish:	Garnish:
watercress	watercress

Place the browning dish in the microwave without the lid, and heat in the microwave empty for 4 minutes. Add the butter and oil then place the pigeons, each wrapped in 2 rashers of bacon, in the heated dish. Cook in the microwave for 4 minutes, turning the birds frequently, so they are browned on all sides. Remove the birds and stir in the onion. Cover and cook in the microwave for 2 minutes. Stir in the flour, redcurrant jelly, wine, stock, tomato purée and seasoning, and return to the microwave for 2 minutes. Stir well and return the birds to the dish. Cover and cook in the microwave for 8 minutes, turning the dish and the birds after 4 minutes. Cook for a further 4 minutes then add the mushrooms, olives and parsley. Cook for 4 minutes. Allow to stand for a few minutes before serving. Garnish with watercress.
Note: If the birds are too high in the dish for the lid to be used, cover with cling film.
Timing of this dish may vary according to the age of the pigeons.

Pigeons in red wine (page 57) in preparation and the finished dish

Meat roasting chart

Instructions for roasting a joint

1. Calculate the cooking time required (see chart).
2. Place the joint on an upturned plate in a large dish. Cook in the microwave for approximately 5 minutes at a time, allowing a 5-minute resting time between each cooking period, until the total microwave cooking time is reached.
3. Wrap in foil (with the shiny side inwards) and stand for 15–30 minutes, or the remaining resting time, until the meat is cooked through.

This is only a guide, as times will vary according to the shape and size of the meat, and also personal taste.

Instructions for defrosting and cooking a frozen joint

1. Weigh the joint to determine the time necessary to defrost it prior to cooking (see chart).
2. Place the joint on an upturned plate in a large dish and defrost in the microwave for approximately 5 minutes at a time, allowing resting periods of 5 minutes between each, until the total calculated defrosting time is reached.
3. Wrap the joint in foil (shiny side inwards) and rest for the remaining suggested resting time, or until the joint is completely thawed.
4. Proceed to cook as for a fresh joint.

Example

Taking a 1.25 kg/2¾ lb (U.S. 2¾ lb) beef topside—frozen.

Total defrosting time	= 16 minutes
Resting time (when defrosting)	= 60 minutes
Total microwave cooking time	= 15 minutes
Resting time (when cooking)	= 35–40 minutes

Following the instructions, place the joint on an upturned plate in a large dish and defrost for four 4-minute periods in the microwave oven, allowing 5-minute resting intervals between each cooking period. Wrap in foil (shiny side inwards) and leave to stand for 45 minutes, or until the joint has defrosted completely.

Unwrap the joint and replace it on the plate then cook in the microwave oven for three periods of 5 minutes, allowing a 5-minute resting interval between each cooking period. Wrap in foil (shiny side inwards) and stand for 25–30 minutes before serving.

Cut of meat

Beef, topside (medium rare)

Beef, rolled rib roast (medium)

Lamb, unboned fillet off leg (well cooked)

Lamb, shoulder boned and rolled (well cooked)

Pork, unboned fillet off leg

POULTRY Chicken, whole, unboned

Duck, whole, unboned

Weight of joint	Total microwave cooking time	Total resting time	Microwave cooking time per 0.5 kg/1 lb	Additional time from frozen		Microwave defrosting time per 0.5 kg/1 lb
				Total microwave defrosting time	Resting time	
1.25 kg/2¾ lb	15 minutes	35–40 minutes	5 minutes	16 minutes	60 minutes	5 minutes
1.5 kg/3 lb	20 minutes	30–40 minutes	6–7 minutes	16 minutes	55 minutes	5 minutes
1 kg/2 lb	15 minutes	35 minutes	7 minutes	9 minutes	35 minutes	4–5 minutes
1.25 kg/2½ lb	20 minutes	30–40 minutes	8 minutes	10 minutes	45–55 minutes	4 minutes
1.5 kg/3 lb	25 minutes	30–40 minutes	8–9 minutes	12 minutes	40–50 minutes	4–5 minutes
1.5 kg/3¼ lb	15 minutes	30 minutes	4½–5 minutes	12 minutes	40 minutes	3½–4 minutes
2 kg/4¾ lb	20 minutes	20 minutes	4–5 minutes	16 minutes	45 minutes	3½–4 minutes

Vegetable dishes

Vegetables are very successfully cooked in the microwave oven, and are often superior in flavour, colour and texture to those cooked by conventional methods. As there is little or no water needed when using a cook-bag, the nutrients are retained (see chart on page 72). Care should be taken when using cook-bags as the steam builds up inside. It is advisable to secure the end of the bag loosely with an elastic band, so that excess steam can escape. Handle the bags carefully, preferably with a tea-towel, to prevent any burning from the steam. Left in the cook-bag the vegetables will remain hot for some time. This is particularly useful when preparing a meal as there is then no need for the vegetables to be reheated.

Vegetables may also be cooked in a suitable dish, preferably covered. The cooking time is then longer as more liquid is required.

The amount of time saved by cooking vegetables in the microwave varies according to the vegetable. Those with a high water content cook more quickly than those with a low water content. Cooking times are also affected by age and size, older vegetables taking longer to cook.

Tuna-stuffed peppers

Utensils: 600-ml/1-pint (U.S. 2½-cup) glass measuring jug, 1-litre/2-pint (U.S. 2½-pint) ovenproof pudding basin, 1-litre/2-pint (U.S. 2½-pint) round shallow ovenproof dish
Microwave cooking time: 24 minutes

Serves: 4

METRIC/IMPERIAL	AMERICAN
100 g/4 oz long grain rice	½ cup long grain rice
300 ml/½ pint hand hot water (about 48°C/120°F)	1¼ cups hand hot water (about 120°F)
½ teaspoon salt	½ teaspoon salt
4 green or red peppers (about 75 g/3 oz each)	4 green or red peppers (about 3 oz each)
50 g/2 oz onion, chopped	½ cup chopped onion
25 g/1 oz butter	2 tablespoons butter
1 (198-g/7-oz) can tuna, drained	1 (7-oz) can tuna, drained
1 tablespoon lemon juice	1 tablespoon lemon juice
100 g/4 oz cucumber, peeled and chopped	1 cup peeled and chopped cucumber
50 g/2 oz mature Cheddar cheese, finely grated	½ cup finely grated strong Cheddar cheese
salt and freshly ground black pepper	salt and freshly ground black pepper

In the measuring jug, mix the rice with the water and salt and cook in the microwave for 10 minutes. Cut the tops off the peppers and remove the seeds and pith from the insides. In the pudding basin, mix the onion and butter and cook in the microwave for 2 minutes. Add the fish, lemon juice, cucumber and cheese. Stir in the cooked rice and season to taste. Pile this mixture into the peppers and place them in the round shallow dish. Pour 150 ml/¼ pint (U.S. ⅔ cup) hand hot water in the dish and cook in the microwave for 12 minutes. Serve with a tomato sauce (see page 76), if liked.

Pork casserole with apple (page 50)

Savoury-stuffed tomatoes

Utensils: 1-litre/2-pint (U.S. 2½-pint) ovenproof pudding basin, 1-litre/2-pint (U.S. 2½-pint) round shallow ovenproof dish, kitchen paper
Microwave cooking time: 3 minutes

Serves: 4

METRIC/IMPERIAL	AMERICAN
4 tomatoes, about 75 g/3 oz each	4 tomatoes, about 3 oz each
100 g/4 oz cooked ham, chopped	½ cup chopped cooked cured ham
50 g/2 oz onion, grated	¼ cup grated onion
25 g/1 oz fresh fine breadcrumbs	¼ cup soft fine bread crumbs
50 g/2 oz mushrooms, chopped	½ cup chopped mushrooms
1 small packet salted crisps, crushed	1 small package salted potato chips, crushed
1 tablespoon grated Parmesan cheese	1 tablespoon grated Parmesan cheese
Garnish:	Garnish:
parsley sprigs	parsley sprigs

Cut the tops off the tomatoes and scoop out the centre flesh. Mix this with the ham, onion, breadcrumbs and mushrooms in the pudding basin and cook in the microwave for 2 minutes. Fill the tomatoes with this mixture and place them in the shallow dish. Prop the tomatoes up if necessary with kitchen paper and heat in the microwave for 1 minute.

Mix together the crushed crisps and Parmesan cheese and sprinkle on top of each tomato. Garnish each with a parsley sprig and serve hot.

Stuffed cabbage leaves

Utensils: 3.5-litre/6-pint (U.S. 7½-pint) ovenproof mixing bowl, 2.25-litre/4-pint (U.S. 5-pint) ovenproof mixing bowl, cook-bag, 600-ml/1-pint (U.S. 2½-cup) glass measuring jug
Microwave cooking time: 14 minutes

Serves: 4

METRIC/IMPERIAL	AMERICAN
8 large cabbage leaves	8 large cabbage leaves
1.75 litres/3 pints hot water	4 pints hot water
Stuffing:	Stuffing:
225 g/8 oz garlic sausage, chopped	½ lb garlic sausage, chopped
50 g/2 oz button mushrooms, chopped	½ cup chopped mushrooms
2 tablespoons grated onion	3 tablespoons grated onion
4 tablespoons fresh brown breadcrumbs	⅓ cup soft brown bread crumbs
1 egg, beaten	1 egg, beaten
salt and freshly ground black pepper	salt and freshly ground black pepper
Sauce:	Sauce:
1 (396-g/14-oz) can tomatoes	1 (14-oz) can tomatoes
1 bay leaf	1 bay leaf
½ teaspoon dried mixed herbs	½ teaspoon dried mixed herbs
1 beef stock cube, crumbled	1 beef bouillon cube, crumbled
2 tablespoons tomato purée	3 tablespoons tomato paste
2 teaspoons cornflour	2 teaspoons cornstarch

Place the cabbage leaves in the larger mixing bowl with the hot water and blanch in the microwave for 3 minutes until they are just cooked. Drain well. In the smaller mixing bowl mix together the ingredients for the stuffing and season lightly. Cook in the microwave for 3 minutes, stirring once.

Divide the stuffing between the cabbage leaves and carefully roll up, folding in the sides of the leaves to form small parcels. Carefully place them in the cook-bag, loosely seal with an elastic band and heat in the microwave for 1 minute, immediately before serving.

Place all the ingredients for the sauce, except the cornflour, in the measuring jug and cook in the microwave for 5 minutes. Strain off the liquid and reserve. Return the sauce to the jug. Blend the cornflour with a little of the reserved liquid and stir into the sauce. In the microwave thicken the sauce for 2 minutes, stirring once, and serve poured over the cabbage leaves.

Sweet and sour red cabbage

Utensil: 2.25-litre/4-pint (U.S. 5-pint) ovenproof mixing bowl
Microwave cooking time: 15 minutes

Serves: 4

METRIC/IMPERIAL	AMERICAN
175 g/6 oz onion, finely chopped	1½ cups finely chopped onion
75 g/3 oz carrot, chopped	¾ cup chopped carrot
75 g/3 oz green pepper, chopped	¾ cup chopped green pepper
100 g/4 oz streaky bacon, chopped	¼ lb bacon slices, chopped
rind and juice of 1 orange	rind and juice of 1 orange
2 tablespoons wine vinegar	3 tablespoons wine vinegar
1 tablespoon soy sauce	1 tablespoon soy sauce
3 tablespoons dry sherry	¼ cup dry sherry
1 heaped tablespoon brown sugar	1 heaped tablespoon brown sugar
2 tablespoons tomato ketchup	3 tablespoons tomato ketchup
450 g/1 lb red cabbage, coarsely shredded	1 lb red cabbage, coarsely shredded
2 teaspoons cornflour	2 teaspoons cornstarch
1 tablespoon water	1 tablespoon water

In the bowl, mix together the onion, carrot, green pepper and bacon and cook in the microwave for 3 minutes. Add the orange rind and juice, wine vinegar, soy sauce, sherry, sugar, tomato ketchup and stir well. Toss the cabbage in the sauce and cook in the microwave for 8 minutes, stirring every 2 minutes.

Blend the cornflour with the water and stir into the cabbage mixture. Thicken in the microwave for a further 4 minutes, stirring twice during cooking.

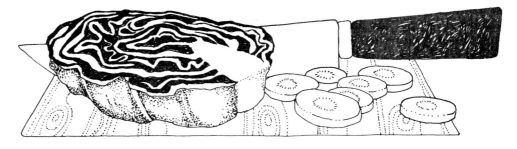

Lyonnaise potatoes

Illustrated on page 83

Utensils: cook-bag, 1.5-litre/2½-pint (U.S. 3-pint) shallow ovenproof dish
Microwave cooking time: 15 minutes

Serves: 4

METRIC/IMPERIAL	AMERICAN
1 medium onion, thinly sliced	1 medium onion, thinly sliced
0.5 kg/1¼ lb potatoes, peeled and sliced 0.25 cm/⅛ inch thick	1¼ lb potatoes, peeled and sliced ⅛ inch thick
salt and freshly ground black pepper	salt and freshly ground black pepper
150 ml/¼ pint double cream	⅔ cup heavy cream
25 g/1 oz cheese, grated	¼ cup grated cheese
Garnish:	Garnish:
few spring onions, sliced	few scallions, sliced

Place the onion in the cook-bag and secure loosely with an elastic band. Make a few snips in the bag to allow the steam to escape. Cook in the microwave for 3 minutes.

Arrange alternate layers of onion and potato in the dish, season and pour over the cream. Cover with cling film and cook in the microwave for 5 minutes. Allow to stand for 1 minute and then continue to cook in the microwave for a further 5 minutes. Remove the cover and sprinkle with grated cheese. Return to the microwave and heat for a further 2 minutes or until the cheese has melted, or place under a hot grill to brown the cheese if preferred.

Stuffed baked potatoes

Utensils: kitchen paper, 1-litre/
  2-pint (U.S. 2½-pint) ovenproof
  soufflé dish
Microwave cooking time: 18–20
  minutes for potatoes (time varies
  for different fillings)

Serves: 4

METRIC/IMPERIAL

4 large potatoes, about 225 g/8 oz each

fillings:
a) Curried prawn
25 g/1 oz butter
2 teaspoons curry powder
50 g/2 oz onion, chopped
2 tablespoons flour
150 ml/¼ pint milk
225 g/8 oz peeled prawns
salt and freshly ground black pepper

b) Celery and cream cheese
225 g/8 oz cream cheese
3 sticks celery, finely chopped
freshly ground black pepper

c) Apple and frankfurter
50 g/2 oz onion, grated
1 large eating apple, chopped
1 (170-g/6-oz) packet frankfurters,
  cut in chunks
¼ teaspoon sage
2 teaspoons cornflour
3 tablespoons water
2 tablespoons double cream
salt and freshly ground black pepper

d) Creamed avocado
2 ripe avocado pears
1 tablespoon lemon juice
2 tablespoons double cream
freshly ground black pepper
chopped chives

AMERICAN

4 large potatoes, about 8 oz each

fillings:
a) Curried prawn or shrimp
2 tablespoons butter
2 teaspoons curry powder
½ cup chopped onion
3 tablespoons all-purpose flour
⅔ cup milk
1 cup peeled prawns or shrimp
salt and freshly ground black pepper

b) Celery and cream cheese
1 cup cream cheese
3 stalks celery, finely chopped
freshly ground black pepper

c) Apple and frankfurter
½ cup grated onion
1 large eating apple, chopped
1 (6-oz) package frankfurters, cut in
  chunks
¼ teaspoon sage
2 teaspoons cornstarch
¼ cup water
3 tablespoons heavy cream
salt and freshly ground black pepper

d) Creamed avocado
2 ripe avocados
1 tablespoon lemon juice
3 tablespoons heavy cream
freshly ground black pepper
chopped chives

Prick the skins of the potatoes and place as far apart as possible on a double thickness of kitchen paper in the microwave oven. Cook for 18–20 minutes, depending on the size of the potatoes, rearranging 4 times during cooking.

Halve the potatoes and top with any of the following fillings:

a) *Curried prawn* In the soufflé dish melt the butter in the microwave for 1 minute. Add the curry powder and onion and cook in the microwave for 5 minutes. Add the flour and mix to a smooth sauce with the milk. Stir in the prawns and continue to cook in the microwave for 5 minutes. Season.

b) *Celery and cream cheese* Mix together the cream cheese and celery, season with pepper and pile on to the halved potatoes immediately before serving.

c) *Apple and frankfurter* In the soufflé dish mix together the onion, apple, frankfurters and sage. Stir well and cook in the microwave for 2 minutes. Blend the cornflour with the water, add the cream and pour over the other ingredients. Heat in the microwave for a further 2 minutes, stirring twice during cooking. Taste and season before serving.

d) *Creamed avocado* Halve the pears, remove the stones and cream the flesh with the lemon juice and cream. Season with freshly ground black pepper and pile on top of the halved potatoes. Sprinkle with chopped chives before serving.

German potato salad

Utensils: cook-bag, 1.5-litre/2½-pint (U.S. 3-pint) oval ovenproof dish
Microwave cooking time: 11 minutes

Serves: 4

METRIC/IMPERIAL	AMERICAN
0.75 kg/1½ lb potatoes, peeled and cut into chunks	1½ lb potatoes, peeled and cut into chunks
4 rashers streaky bacon, chopped	4 bacon slices, chopped
½ bunch spring onions, finely sliced	½ bunch scallions, finely sliced
25 g/1 oz butter	2 tablespoons butter
1 tablespoon flour	1 tablespoon all-purpose flour
salt and freshly ground black pepper	salt and freshly ground black pepper
100 g/4 oz garlic sausage, cubed	¼ lb garlic sausage, cubed
150 ml/¼ pint single cream	⅔ cup light cream
Garnish:	Garnish:
poppy seeds	poppy seeds
chopped chives	chopped chives

Place the chunks of potato in the cook-bag and secure loosely with an elastic band. Make several snips in the bag, to allow the steam to escape. Cook in the microwave for 5 minutes and leave in the bag to keep hot.

Place the bacon, onions and butter in the oval dish and cook in the microwave for 5 minutes. Stir in the flour, seasoning, garlic sausage and cream and heat in the microwave for 1 minute. Stir in the cooked potatoes and sprinkle with poppy seeds and chopped chives.

Cream-baked cucumber

Utensil: 1.5-litre/2½-pint (U.S. 3-pint) oval ovenproof dish
Microwave cooking time: 10 minutes

Serves: 4

METRIC/IMPERIAL	AMERICAN
1 cucumber, peeled	1 cucumber, peeled
½ teaspoon dill weed	½ teaspoon dill weed
150 ml/¼ pint double cream	⅔ cup heavy cream
salt and freshly ground black pepper	salt and freshly ground black pepper
4 tablespoons chopped chives	⅓ cup chopped chives

Quarter the cucumber lengthwise then cut into pieces approximately 5–7.5 cm/2–3 inches long. Place the pieces of cucumber in the oval dish. Sprinkle on the dill weed and pour the cream over the cucumber. Season lightly and cook in the microwave for 10 minutes. Sprinkle with chopped chives and serve hot.

Courgettes à la grecque

Utensil: 1.5-litre/2½-pint (U.S. 3-pint) oval ovenproof dish
Microwave cooking time: 7 minutes

Serves: 4

METRIC/IMPERIAL	AMERICAN
2 tablespoons oil	3 tablespoons oil
25 g/1 oz butter	2 tablespoons butter
0.5 kg/1 lb courgettes, sliced	1 lb zucchini, sliced
2 cloves garlic, crushed	2 cloves garlic, crushed
4 tomatoes, skinned and sliced	4 tomatoes, skinned and sliced
100 g/4 oz button mushrooms	1 cup button mushrooms
Garnish:	Garnish:
chopped parsley	chopped parsley

Place the oil and butter in the oval dish and melt in the microwave for 1 minute. Add the courgettes and garlic and mix well. Cover with cling film and cook in the microwave for 2 minutes. Stir in the tomatoes and mushrooms, cover and cook in the microwave for a further 2 minutes. Stir the vegetables thoroughly, bringing the outside vegetables to the centre of the dish and vice versa. Cover and continue to cook in the microwave for a further 2 minutes. Allow to cool slightly before serving.

Garnish with chopped parsley.

Spinach au gratin

Utensils: cook-bag, 1-litre/1½-pint
   (U.S. 2-pint) oblong ovenproof dish
Microwave cooking time:
   11 minutes

Serves: 4

METRIC/IMPERIAL
0.5 kg/1 lb spinach, washed, dried
   and shredded
1 small onion, grated
25 g/1 oz butter
salt and freshly ground black pepper
pinch freshly ground nutmeg
3 tomatoes, skinned and sliced
150 ml/¼ pint double cream
Garnish:
grated Parmesan cheese
chopped parsley

AMERICAN
1 lb spinach, washed, dried and
   shredded
1 small onion, grated
2 tablespoons butter
salt and freshly ground black pepper
pinch freshly ground nutmeg
3 tomatoes, skinned and sliced
⅔ cup heavy cream
Garnish:
grated Parmesan cheese
chopped parsley

Place the spinach in the cook-bag and secure loosely with an elastic band. Make several snips in the bag to allow the steam to escape. Cook in the microwave for 4 minutes. Place the onion and half the butter in the oval dish and cook in the microwave for 4 minutes. Add the spinach, small pieces of the remaining butter and seasoning. Top with the sliced tomatoes and pour over the cream. Heat in the microwave for 3 minutes. Allow to stand for a few minutes before serving. Garnish with Parmesan cheese and chopped parsley.

Cauliflower provençal

Utensil: 1.5-litre/2½-pint (U.S.
   3-pint) round ovenproof dish
Microwave cooking time:
   20 minutes

Serves: 4

METRIC/IMPERIAL
1 cauliflower
1 tablespoon oil
1 clove garlic, crushed
1 small onion, finely chopped
1 (397-g/14-oz) can tomatoes
salt and freshly ground black pepper
few drops Worcestershire sauce
1 teaspoon chopped fresh marjoram
75 g/3 oz Cheddar cheese, grated
Garnish:
chopped parsley

AMERICAN
1 cauliflower
1 tablespoon oil
1 clove garlic, crushed
1 small onion, finely chopped
1 (14-oz) can tomatoes
salt and freshly ground black pepper
few drops Worcestershire sauce
1 teaspoon chopped fresh marjoram
¾ cup grated Cheddar cheese
Garnish:
chopped parsley

Divide the cauliflower into small sprigs and place in the ovenproof dish. Pour over 600 ml/1 pint (2½ cups) boiling water and cook in the microwave for 5 minutes. Drain well.

Using the same dish, add the oil, garlic and onion and cook in the microwave for 3 minutes. Stir in the tomatoes, seasoning, Worcestershire sauce, herbs and drained cauliflower. Cover and continue to cook for 10 minutes, stirring once during cooking. Sprinkle the cheese over the top and return to the microwave for 2 minutes until the cheese has melted. If liked, it can be browned under a conventional grill just before serving. Garnish with chopped parsley.

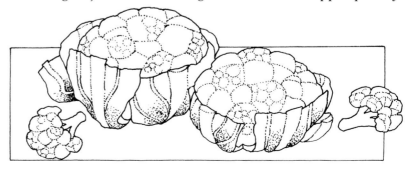

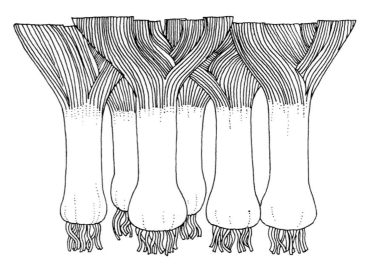

Leeks in creamy wine sauce

Utensils: cook-bag, ovenproof
   serving dish, 300-ml/½-pint
   (U.S. 1¼-cup) glass measuring jug
Microwave cooking time: 9 minutes

Serves: 4

METRIC/IMPERIAL	AMERICAN
0.75 kg/1½ lb leeks, washed and trimmed	1½ lb leeks, washed and trimmed
150 ml/¼ pint dry white wine	⅔ cup dry white wine
150 ml/¼ pint boiling chicken stock	⅔ cup boiling chicken stock
3 teaspoons cornflour	3 teaspoons cornstarch
3 tablespoons double cream	¼ cup heavy cream
salt and freshly ground black pepper	salt and freshly ground black pepper

Slice the leeks and place in the cook-bag with the wine. Seal loosely with an elastic band and cook in the microwave for 6 minutes.

Strain the leeks, reserving the cooking liquid, and place in the serving dish. Pour the cooking liquid into the measuring jug together with the stock. Blend the cornflour with the cream and stir into the stock. Season and thicken in the microwave for 3 minutes, stirring twice during cooking. Pour over the leeks before serving.

Asparagus in lemon butter

Illustrated overleaf

Utensils: cook-bag, 1-litre/2-pint
   (U.S. 2½-pint) pudding basin
Microwave cooking time:
   10–12 minutes

Serves: 4

METRIC/IMPERIAL	AMERICAN
450 g/1 lb asparagus	1 lb asparagus
2 tablespoons hot water	3 tablespoons hot water
100 g/4 oz butter	½ cup butter
juice of ½ lemon	juice of ½ lemon
salt and freshly ground black pepper	salt and freshly ground black pepper
grated Parmesan cheese (optional)	grated Parmesan cheese (optional)

Trim off all the white woody part of the asparagus to give even-length spears weighing approximately 350 g/12 oz.

Lay the spears flat in the cook-bag, making sure that the trimmed ends do not overlap. Spoon the water into the bag and seal loosely with an elastic band. Cook in the microwave for 5–7 minutes. Carefully open the bag and test the asparagus with a knife. Cooking time may vary a little with the thickness and age of the asparagus.

Place the butter and lemon juice in the pudding basin and season well. Melt in the microwave for 5 minutes and pour over the asparagus before serving. Sprinkle with a little Parmesan cheese, if liked.
Note: If the asparagus is left in the cook-bag with the elastic band on, it will keep hot for up to 10 minutes.

Vegetable cooking chart

Vegetable	Quantity or weight	Cooking utensil	Quantity of water or butter used	Microwave cooking time
Artichokes, globe	1 medium	cook-bag	4 tablespoons (U.S. $\frac{1}{3}$ cup) water	8–10 minutes
Artichokes, Jerusalem	450 g/1 lb peeled	cook-bag	2 tablespoons (U.S. 3 tablespoons) lemon juice, 25 g/1 oz (U.S. 2 tablespoons) butter	10–12 minutes
Asparagus	450 g/1 lb medium spears, trimmed	cook-bag	2 tablespoons (U.S. 3 tablespoons) water	5–7 minutes
Beans, broad	450 g/1 lb (shelled weight)	cook-bag	2 tablespoons (U.S. 3 tablespoons) water	5–7 minutes
Beans, French	450 g/1 lb	cook-bag	3 tablespoons (U.S. $\frac{1}{4}$ cup) water	7–8 minutes
Beans, runner	450 g/1 lb sliced	cook-bag	3 tablespoons (U.S. $\frac{1}{4}$ cup) water	5–7 minutes
Beetroot	4 medium	cook-bag	4 tablespoons (U.S. $\frac{1}{3}$ cup) water	10 minutes
Broccoli	450 g/1 lb	cook-bag	3 tablespoons (U.S. $\frac{1}{4}$ cup) water	7–8 minutes
Cabbage	450 g/1 lb shredded	cook-bag	2 tablespoons (U.S. 3 tablespoons) water	10 minutes
Carrots	225 g/8 oz in 1-cm/$\frac{1}{2}$-inch slices	cook-bag	2 tablespoons (U.S. 3 tablespoons) water	5 minutes
Cauliflower	225 g/8 oz broken in florets	cook-bag	4 tablespoons (U.S. $\frac{1}{3}$ cup) water	5 minutes

Vegetable	Quantity or weight	Cooking utensil	Quantity of water or butter used	Microwave cooking time
Corn on the cob	2 cobs, with husks removed	cook-bag	3 tablespoons (U.S. ¼ cup) water	8–10 minutes
Courgettes	450 g/1 lb sliced	cook-bag	25 g/1 oz (U.S. 2 tablespoons) butter	3 minutes plus 10 minutes standing time
Leeks	450 g/1 lb sliced	cook-bag	25 g/1 oz (U.S. 2 tablespoons) butter	5–7 minutes
Mushrooms, button	225 g/8 oz whole	cook-bag	25 g/1 oz (U.S. 2 tablespoons) butter	1½ minutes
Onions, whole	175 g/6 oz each (2 at a time)	cook-bag	2 tablespoons (U.S. 3 tablespoons) water	10 minutes
Parsnips	450 g/1 lb sliced	cook-bag	2 tablespoons (U.S. 3 tablespoons) water	10 minutes
Peas	450 g/1 lb (shelled weight)	cook-bag	2 tablespoons (U.S. 3 tablespoons) water	8 minutes
Potatoes, baked	1 kg/2 lb (4 large, even-sized)	on kitchen paper	—	18–20 minutes
Potatoes, boiled	450 g/1 lb (in 50-g/ 2-oz pieces)	cook-bag	3 tablespoons (U.S. ¼ cup) water	5–7 minutes
Potatoes, new	450 g/1 lb (even-sized)	cook-bag	4 tablespoons (U.S. ⅓ cup) water	5 minutes
Spinach	450 g/1 lb	cook-bag	—	5–6 minutes
Spring greens	450 g/1 lb	cook-bag	—	8 minutes
Swede	450 g/1 lb (in 25-g/1-oz pieces)	cook-bag	2 tablespoons (U.S. 3 tablespoons) water	10 minutes

Sauces, sweet and savoury

Sauces cooked in the microwave are always foolproof. No more burnt saucepans to wash up!

It is, however, important to use the recommended size of measuring jug or basin, as stated in the recipe. The sauce could boil over if too small a basin is used.

Most of these sauces can be made in advance and then reheated in the microwave just before serving. It really is worthwhile taking the trouble to make a sauce as it can add that special finishing touch to a dish.

Cumberland sauce

Utensil: 1-litre/2-pint (U.S. 2½-pint) ovenproof pudding basin
Microwave cooking time: 5 minutes

Makes: 450 ml/¾ pint (U.S. 2 cups)

METRIC/IMPERIAL
2 tablespoons soft brown sugar
pinch cayenne pepper
150 ml/¼ pint hot chicken stock, made with a stock cube
150 ml/¼ pint red wine
1 tablespoon cornflour
3 tablespoons redcurrant jelly
grated rind of ½ small orange
2 tablespoons orange juice
salt and freshly ground black pepper

AMERICAN
3 tablespoons light brown sugar
pinch cayenne pepper
⅔ cup hot chicken stock, made with a bouillon cube
⅔ cup red wine
1 tablespoon cornstarch
¼ cup red currant jelly
grated rind of ½ small orange
3 tablespoons orange juice
salt and freshly ground black pepper

Place the sugar, cayenne, chicken stock and wine in the pudding basin and cook in the microwave for 3 minutes. Blend the cornflour with a little cold water and stir into the sauce. Add the remaining ingredients and continue to cook in the microwave for 2 minutes. This sauce makes an excellent accompaniment to gammon or pork dishes.

Tomato sauce (page 76) and Cumberland sauce

Tomato sauce

Illustrated on page 74

Utensil: 1-litre/2-pint (U.S. 2½-pint) ovenproof pudding basin
Microwave cooking time: 7 minutes

Makes: 450 ml/¾ pint (U.S. 2 cups)

METRIC/IMPERIAL	AMERICAN
15 g/½ oz butter	1 tablespoon butter
1 small onion, finely chopped	1 small onion, finely chopped
25 g/1 oz flour	¼ cup all-purpose flour
1 (396-g/14-oz) can tomatoes	1 (14-oz) can tomatoes
pinch basil	pinch basil
few drops Worcestershire sauce	few drops Worcestershire sauce
salt and freshly ground black pepper	salt and freshly ground black pepper
150 ml/¼ pint red wine	⅔ cup red wine
1 chicken stock cube, crumbled	1 chicken bouillon cube, crumbled
2 tablespoons tomato purée	3 tablespoons tomato paste
1 tablespoon chopped parsley (optional)	1 tablespoon chopped parsley (optional)

Place the butter and chopped onion in the pudding basin and cook in the microwave for 2 minutes, stirring once during cooking. Stir in the flour, then add the remaining ingredients. Return to the microwave for 5 minutes, stirring twice. Allow to cool slightly before liquidising. Reheat in the microwave if necessary.

Sweet 'n' sour sauce

Utensil: 2.25-litre/4-pint (U.S. 5-pint) ovenproof mixing bowl
Microwave cooking time: 12 minutes

Makes: 750 ml/1¼ pints (U.S. 3 cups)

METRIC/IMPERIAL	AMERICAN
2 tablespoons oil	3 tablespoons oil
100 g/4 oz onion, coarsely chopped	1 cup coarsely chopped onion
100 g/4 oz green pepper, coarsely chopped	1 cup coarsely chopped green pepper
100 g/4 oz carrots, cut into strips	¼ lb carrots, cut into strips
6 tablespoons tomato ketchup	½ cup tomato ketchup
2 tablespoons soy sauce	3 tablespoons soy sauce
3 tablespoons dry sherry	¼ cup dry sherry
2 tablespoons wine vinegar	3 tablespoons wine vinegar
1 (226-g/8-oz) can pineapple chunks	1 (8-oz) can pineapple chunks
1 tablespoon brown sugar	1 tablespoon brown sugar

Heat the oil in the mixing bowl in the microwave for 2 minutes then add the onion, pepper and carrot and continue to cook in the microwave for a further 5 minutes. Stir in all the remaining ingredients and cook in the microwave for a further 5 minutes.

Serve this tangy sauce with cooked pork, lamb, poultry or fish.

Hot barbecue sauce

Utensil: 1-litre/2-pint (U.S. 2½-pint) ovenproof pudding basin
Microwave cooking time: 9 minutes

Makes: 200 ml/7 fl oz (U.S. ¾ cup)

METRIC/IMPERIAL	AMERICAN
1 small onion, grated	1 small onion, grated
4 tablespoons tomato purée	⅓ cup tomato paste
150 ml/¼ pint water	⅔ cup water
1 tablespoon wine vinegar	1 tablespoon wine vinegar
1 tablespoon Worcestershire sauce	1 tablespoon Worcestershire sauce
2 teaspoons brown sugar	2 teaspoons light brown sugar
salt and freshly ground black pepper	salt and freshly ground black pepper
2 tablespoons redcurrant jelly	3 tablespoons red currant jelly

Place all the ingredients together in the pudding basin and cook in the microwave for 9 minutes, stirring 3 times during cooking.

This sauce is delicious served with pork or lamb dishes.

Curry sauce

Utensil: 1.5-litre/2½-pint (U.S. 3-
  pint) ovenproof basin
Microwave cooking time:
  14 minutes

Makes: 450 ml/¾ pint
  (U.S. 2 cups)

METRIC/IMPERIAL	AMERICAN
1 onion, finely chopped	1 onion, finely chopped
1 clove garlic, crushed	1 clove garlic, crushed
25 g/1 oz butter	2 tablespoons butter
1 tablespoon oil	1 tablespoon oil
3 tablespoons curry powder	¼ cup curry powder
1 tablespoon flour	1 tablespoon all-purpose flour
2 tablespoons tomato purée	3 tablespoons tomato paste
pinch ground cloves	pinch ground cloves
2 tablespoons chutney	3 tablespoons chutney or relish
pinch cayenne pepper	pinch cayenne pepper
salt and freshly ground black pepper	salt and freshly ground black pepper
1 teaspoon lemon juice	1 teaspoon lemon juice
1 teaspoon black treacle	1 teaspoon molasses
450 ml/¾ pint hot chicken stock	2 cups hot chicken stock
few drops Worcestershire sauce	few drops Worcestershire sauce

Place the onion, garlic, butter and oil in the basin and cook in the microwave for 4 minutes, stirring twice during the cooking time. Stir in the remaining ingredients and continue to cook in the microwave for 10 minutes, stirring frequently. Serve with all meat, fish or egg dishes.

Bread sauce

Utensil: 600-ml/1-pint (U.S. 2½-cup)
  glass measuring jug
Microwave cooking time:
  5–6 minutes

Makes: 300 ml/½ pint
  (U.S. 1¼ cups)

METRIC/IMPERIAL	AMERICAN
1 small onion, studded with 6 cloves	1 small onion, studded with 6 cloves
300 ml/½ pint milk	1¼ cups milk
75 g/3 oz fresh breadcrumbs	1½ cups fresh soft bread crumbs
25 g/1 oz butter	2 tablespoons butter

Place the onion and the milk in the measuring jug and cook in the microwave for 4 minutes. Remove the onion and stir in the breadcrumbs and butter. Stand for 30 minutes. Reheat in the microwave for 1–2 minutes. Serve bread sauce with game and poultry dishes, especially at Christmas time.

White sauce with variations

Utensil: 600-ml/1-pint (U.S. 2½-cup) glass measuring jug
Microwave cooking time: 5 minutes

Makes: 300 ml/½ pint
    (U.S. 1¼ cups)

METRIC/IMPERIAL	AMERICAN
25 g/1 oz butter	2 tablespoons butter
25 g/1 oz flour	¼ cup all-purpose flour
300 ml/½ pint milk	1¼ cups milk
salt and freshly ground black pepper	salt and freshly ground black pepper

Melt the butter in the measuring jug in the microwave for 1 minute. Stir in the flour until well mixed then pour in the milk and stir well. Cook in the microwave for 4 minutes, stirring after every minute to prevent lumps forming. Season to taste.

Variations

Cheese sauce Stir 50 g/2 oz (U.S. ½ cup) grated cheese into the cooked sauce.
Anchovy sauce Add 1–2 tablespoons anchovy essence to the cooked sauce.
Parsley sauce Stir 2–3 tablespoons (U.S. 3–4 tablespoons) chopped parsley into the cooked sauce.
Mushroom sauce Stir 50 g/2 oz (U.S. ½ cup) chopped cooked mushrooms into the cooked sauce.

Onion sauce

Utensil: 1-litre/2-pint (U.S. 2½-pint) ovenproof pudding basin
Microwave cooking time: 9 minutes

Makes: 300 ml/½ pint
    (U.S. 1¼ cups)

METRIC/IMPERIAL	AMERICAN
25 g/1 oz butter	2 tablespoons butter
1 large onion, thinly sliced	1 large onion, thinly sliced
25 g/1 oz flour	¼ cup all-purpose flour
300 ml/½ pint milk	1¼ cups milk
salt and freshly ground black pepper	salt and freshly ground black pepper

Place the butter and onion slices in the basin and cook in the microwave for 6 minutes, stirring twice during cooking. Stir in the flour, then add the milk and mix well. Return to the microwave for 3 minutes, stirring once. Season to taste. Onion sauce is delicious with lamb dishes.

Béchamel sauce

Utensil: 600-ml/1-pint (U.S. 2½-cup) glass measuring jug
Microwave cooking time:
    8–9 minutes

Makes: 300 ml/½ pint
    (U.S. 1¼ cups)

METRIC/IMPERIAL	AMERICAN
1 small onion, quartered	1 small onion, quartered
1 carrot, thickly sliced	1 carrot, thickly sliced
1 bay leaf	1 bay leaf
mace	mace
10 peppercorns	10 peppercorns
few sprigs parsley	few sprigs parsley
300 ml/½ pint milk	1¼ cups milk
25 g/1 oz butter	2 tablespoons butter
25 g/1 oz flour	¼ cup all-purpose flour
salt and freshly ground black pepper	salt and freshly ground black pepper

Place the vegetables, bay leaf, mace, peppercorns, parsley and milk in the measuring jug and cook in the microwave for 4 minutes, or until the milk comes to the boil. Infuse for 30 minutes then strain.

Place the butter in the measuring jug and melt in the microwave for 1 minute. Stir in the flour, mixing well, and then stir in the strained milk. Return to the microwave for 3–4 minutes, until thickened, stirring every minute. Season to taste.

Somerset pork with cider cream sauce
(page 49)

Apple sauce

Utensil: 1-litre/2-pint (U.S. 2½-pint) ovenproof pudding basin
Microwave cooking time: 2½ minutes

Makes: 300 ml/½ pint (U.S. 1¼ cups)

METRIC/IMPERIAL
450 g/1 lb cooking apples, peeled, cored and sliced
2 tablespoons water
25 g/1 oz butter

AMERICAN
1 lb cooking apples, peeled, cored and sliced
3 tablespoons water
2 tablespoons butter

Place all the ingredients in the pudding basin and cook in the microwave for 2½ minutes, stirring once during cooking. Sieve or mash the sauce until smooth. Serve with pork dishes and roast duck.

Brandy sauce

Utensil: 600-ml/1-pint (U.S. 2½-cup) glass measuring jug
Microwave cooking time: 2½ minutes

Makes: 300 ml/½ pint (U.S. 1¼ cups)

METRIC/IMPERIAL
25 g/1 oz cornflour
300 ml/½ pint milk
25 g/1 oz castor sugar
15 g/½ oz butter
1 tablespoon brandy

AMERICAN
¼ cup cornstarch
1¼ cups milk
2 tablespoons sugar
1 tablespoon butter
1 tablespoon brandy

Blend the cornflour with a little of the milk until smooth. Place the remaining milk in the measuring jug and heat in the microwave for 1 minute. Pour on to the blended cornflour and then return to the jug. Cook in the microwave for 1½ minutes, whisking after 1 minute. Add the sugar, butter and brandy, and whisk until smooth.

Chocolate sauce

Utensil: 1.75-litre/3-pint (U.S. 4-pint) ovenproof pudding basin
Microwave cooking time: 2½ minutes

Makes: 300 ml/½ pint (U.S. 1¼ cups)

METRIC/IMPERIAL
100 g/4 oz plain cooking chocolate
5 tablespoons golden syrup
3 tablespoons cocoa powder
3 tablespoons warm water
1 oz butter, melted

AMERICAN
4 squares semi-sweet cooking chocolate
6 tablespoons corn syrup
¼ cup unsweetened cocoa powder
¼ cup warm water
2 tablespoons melted butter

Place the chocolate, broken into pieces, with the syrup in the pudding basin, and melt in the microwave for 2 minutes. In a separate basin, blend the cocoa powder with the water and butter. Add to the chocolate mixture and cook in the microwave for a further 30 seconds.

Custard sauce

Utensil: 600-ml/1-pint (U.S. 2½-cup) glass measuring jug
Microwave cooking time: 7 minutes

Makes: 300 ml/½ pint (U.S. 1¼ cups)

METRIC/IMPERIAL
300 ml/½ pint milk
2 eggs
1 tablespoon castor sugar
few drops vanilla essence

AMERICAN
1¼ cups milk
2 eggs
1 tablespoon sugar
few drops vanilla extract

Heat the milk in the measuring jug in the microwave for 3 minutes, or until *just* boiling. Lightly whisk the eggs, sugar and essence. Pour the milk on to the whisked mixture, mix well and strain back into the jug. Return to the microwave for 4 minutes, standing the jug in a waterbath of hand hot tap water, stirring every minute. The custard should lightly coat the back of a spoon when cooked.

Egg and cheese dishes

Egg and cheese dishes cook particularly well in the microwave oven. Most of the recipes in this chapter take 10 minutes or less to cook, thus providing some good ideas for snacks.

There are two important points to remember when cooking eggs in the microwave. Firstly, you cannot boil eggs in their shells as they will burst, and secondly, foods that are egg and breadcrumbed become leathery.

Care must be taken not to overcook egg and cheese dishes as they can quickly become indigestible.

Kipper soufflé

Utensils: 1.5-litre/2½-pint (U.S. 3-pint) shallow oblong ovenproof dish, 3.5-litre/6-pint (U.S. 7½-pint) ovenproof mixing bowl, 600-ml/1-pint (U.S. 2½-cup) glass measuring jug
Microwave cooking time: 10 minutes

Serves: 4–6

METRIC/IMPERIAL	AMERICAN
225 g/8 oz frozen kipper fillets	½ lb frozen kipper fillets
1 small onion, chopped	1 small onion, chopped
grated rind of 1 lemon	grated rind of 1 lemon
1 tablespoon lemon juice	1 tablespoon lemon juice
50 g/2 oz butter	¼ cup butter
50 g/2 oz flour	½ cup all-purpose flour
600 ml/1 pint milk	2½ cups milk
1 tablespoon chopped parsley	1 tablespoon chopped parsley
4 eggs, separated	4 eggs, separated
salt and freshly ground black pepper	salt and freshly ground black pepper
15 g/½ oz gelatine	2 envelopes gelatin
1 tablespoon hot water	1 tablespoon hot water
Garnish:	Garnish:
chopped parsley	chopped parsley
quartered lemon slices	quartered lemon slices

Place the frozen kipper fillets in the oblong dish together with the onion, lemon rind and juice. Cook in the microwave for 3 minutes then turn the fish over and cook for a further 3 minutes.

Melt the butter in the mixing bowl in the microwave for 1 minute then stir in the flour. Heat the milk in the measuring jug in the microwave for 3 minutes then stir into the flour and butter. Whisk thoroughly and return to the microwave for 3 minutes, whisking every minute. Allow to cool slightly.

Remove the skin from the fish and liquidise the fish with the onion and any juices together with a little of the white sauce. Whisk the fish mixture, parsley and egg yolks into the sauce, taste and season.

Dissolve the gelatine in the hot water and whisk into the fish mixture then chill until half set. Meanwhile, prepare a 14-cm/5½-inch soufflé dish by tying a double band of greaseproof paper around the side of the dish to rise 5 cm/2 inches above the edge of the dish. Secure firmly.

Whisk the egg whites until they form stiff peaks then fold into the half set fish mixture and pour into the prepared soufflé dish. Allow to set then carefully remove the greaseproof paper. Press the chopped parsley around the sides of the soufflé and garnish the top with quartered lemon slices.

Baked Vienna eggs

*Utensil: 24-cm/9½-inch round
ovenproof plate*
*Microwave cooking time:
4–4½ minutes*

Serves: 4

METRIC/IMPERIAL	AMERICAN
4 crisp Vienna rolls	4 crisp Vienna rolls
4 short rashers bacon	4 slices Canadian bacon
4 standard eggs	4 eggs
salt and freshly ground black pepper	salt and freshly ground black pepper

Cut the top off each roll and hollow out the soft bread from the centre. Line each roll with a rasher of bacon and crack an egg into the cavity. Season lightly and place 2 rolls on the plate. Cook 2 rolls at a time in the microwave for 2 minutes to 2 minutes 15 seconds depending on how well cooked the egg is liked.
Note: The bread scooped out from the rolls may be made into breadcrumbs and dried or frozen for later use.

Scrambled eggs suprême

*Utensil: 1.75-litre/3-pint (U.S. 4-
pint) ovenproof pudding basin*
Microwave cooking time: 4 minutes

Serves: 4

METRIC/IMPERIAL	AMERICAN
6 eggs	6 eggs
50 g/2 oz button mushrooms, chopped	½ cup chopped mushrooms
25 g/1 oz cheese, grated	¼ cup grated cheese
75 g/3 oz garlic sausage, chopped	scant ½ cup chopped garlic sausage
3 tablespoons double cream	¼ cup heavy cream
salt and freshly ground black pepper	salt and freshly ground black pepper

Whisk the eggs in the pudding basin, add the mushrooms and cook in the microwave for 1 minute, stirring once.
   Add the cheese, garlic sausage and cream, season lightly and return to the microwave for 3 minutes, stirring every minute, until almost set. Stir well and leave for 1 minute before serving with hot buttered toast.

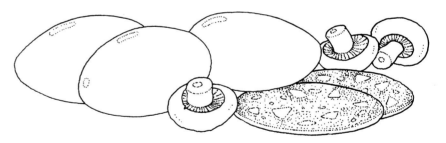

Stilton-baked eggs

*Utensils: 4 150-ml/¼-pint (U.S. ⅔-
cup) ovenproof ramekin dishes*
Microwave cooking time: 3 minutes

Serves: 4

METRIC/IMPERIAL	AMERICAN
1 (170-g/6-oz) packet frozen chopped spinach, thawed	1 (6-oz) package frozen chopped spinach, thawed
100 g/4 oz Stilton cheese, crumbled	1 cup crumbled Stilton or other blue cheese
4 standard eggs	4 eggs
little grated nutmeg	little grated nutmeg

Divide the spinach between the 4 ramekin dishes. Reserve a little of the Stilton cheese and sprinkle the rest in the ramekins on top of the spinach. Break an egg in each dish and sprinkle with a little nutmeg. Sprinkle the remaining cheese over the eggs and cook two at a time in the microwave for 1½ minutes, checking the eggs after 1 minute. Serve hot with Melba toast.
Note: When cooking eggs in the microwave oven the timing is particularly critical, as the eggs should be removed before they are completely cooked.

Lyonnaise potatoes (page 65)

Scotch eggs in herby cheese sauce

Utensils: 1-litre/2-pint (U.S. 2½-pint) shallow round ovenproof dish, 600-ml/1-pint (U.S. 2½-cup) glass measuring jug

Microwave cooking time: 6 minutes

Serves: 4

METRIC/IMPERIAL	AMERICAN
225 g/8 oz sausagemeat	1 cup sausage meat
75 g/3 oz onion, grated	¾ cup grated onion
4 hard-boiled eggs, shelled	4 hard-cooked eggs, shelled
50 g/2 oz fresh brown breadcrumbs	1 cup soft brown bread crumbs
1 tablespoon flour	1 tablespoon all-purpose flour
300 ml/½ pint milk	1¼ cups milk
100 g/4 oz cheese, finely grated	1 cup finely grated cheese
1 teaspoon mixed herbs	1 teaspoon mixed herbs
salt and freshly ground black pepper	salt and freshly ground black pepper
Garnish:	Garnish:
tomato wedges	tomato wedges
watercress	watercress

Mix the sausagemeat with the grated onion and divide into 4 pieces. On a floured board, Wrap each egg evenly in sausagemeat. Roll the eggs in the breadcrumbs and place, as far apart as possible, in the round dish. Cook in the microwave for 3 minutes, turning the dish and eggs round 3–4 times during cooking.

In the measuring jug, blend the flour with a little of the milk and gradually whisk in the rest of the milk. Stir in the cheese and herbs and heat in the microwave for 3 minutes, whisking twice during cooking and at the end of the cooking time. Season and taste the sauce before pouring over the Scotch eggs. Garnish with wedges of tomatoes and sprigs of watercress before serving.
Note: Eggs may *NOT* be boiled in the microwave oven as steam builds up within the shell and causes the egg to explode.

Coating with egg and breadcrumbs in the traditional manner is unsuccessful in the microwave oven as the egg coating hardens, becoming rubbery and unpleasant.

Cheesy flowerpot loaves

Illustrated on pages 86–87

Utensils: 6 7.5-cm/3-inch clay flowerpots

Microwave cooking time: 9 minutes

Makes: 6

METRIC/IMPERIAL	AMERICAN
175 g/6 oz brown wholewheat flour	1½ cups brown wholewheat flour
25 g/1 oz wheat bran	¼ cup wheat bran
½ teaspoon salt	½ teaspoon salt
½ teaspoon dry mustard	½ teaspoon dry mustard
50 g/2 oz Farmhouse English Cheddar cheese, finely grated	½ cup finely grated strong Cheddar cheese
1½ teaspoons dried yeast	1½ teaspoons active dry yeast
1 teaspoon sugar	1 teaspoon sugar
300 ml/½ pint tepid water	1¼ cups tepid water
1 egg, beaten	1 egg, beaten

In a mixing bowl, mix together the brown flour, bran, salt, mustard and cheese. Dissolve the dried yeast with the sugar in the water and leave in a warm place until it becomes frothy. Whisk in the beaten egg.

Mix the yeast liquid into the dry ingredients and beat well to form a soft mixture. Place a small round of greaseproof paper in the base of each flowerpot to cover the hole. Divide the mixture between the 6 flowerpots and cover with a piece of polythene or cling film. Leave in a warm place until the mixture has almost doubled in size.

Uncover the pots and cook in the microwave two at a time, allowing 3 minutes for each pair. When cooked, slide a knife between the bread and the flowerpot and turn out on to a wire rack to cool. Remove the greaseproof paper from the base of the breads. Serve with butter and cheese or instead of conventional rolls.

Note: These are best eaten on the day they are made.

Variations

Herby cheese flowerpot loaves Add 2 teaspoons dried mixed herbs to the dry ingredients then proceed as for the basic recipe.

Nutty cheese flowerpot loaves Add 50 g/2 oz (U.S. ½ cup) chopped walnuts to the dry ingredients then proceed as for the basic recipe.

Cheesy fruit flowerpot loaves Add 50 g/2 oz (U.S. ⅓ cup) sultanas to the dry ingredients then proceed as for the basic recipe.

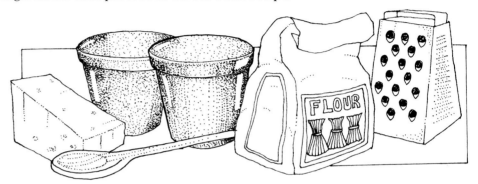

Mixed vegetables au gratin

Utensils: cook-bag, 2.25-litre/4-pint (U.S. 5-pint) deep oblong ovenproof dish
Microwave cooking time: 19 minutes

Serves: 4–6

METRIC/IMPERIAL	AMERICAN
350 g/12 oz cauliflower florets	12 oz cauliflower florets
2 tablespoons water	3 tablespoons water
1 large onion, thinly sliced	1 large onion, thinly sliced
1 large green pepper, cut in rings	1 large green pepper, cut in rings
25 g/1 oz butter	2 tablespoons butter
2 medium beetroot, cooked and chopped	2 medium beets, cooked and chopped
salt and freshly ground black pepper	salt and freshly ground black pepper
150 ml/¼ pint double cream	⅔ cup heavy cream
¼ teaspoon lemon juice	¼ teaspoon lemon juice
1 clove garlic, crushed	1 clove garlic, crushed
100 g/4 oz mature Cheddar cheese, grated	1 cup grated strong Cheddar cheese
50 g/2 oz fresh brown breadcrumbs	1 cup soft brown bread crumbs
2 hard-boiled eggs, chopped	2 hard-cooked eggs, chopped
1 tablespoon chopped parsley	1 tablespoon chopped parsley

Place the cauliflower and water in the cook-bag, secure the end loosely with an elastic band and cook in the microwave for 5 minutes. Remove the cauliflower to a strainer and place the onion and green pepper in the bag with the butter. Secure the end with the elastic band, again allowing room for the steam to escape, and cook in the microwave for 8 minutes. Shake the bag twice during cooking.

Place the beetroot in the bottom of the oblong dish and arrange the onion and pepper on top, pouring over the butter from the cook-bag. Place the cauliflower florets on top and season well.

Mix the cream and lemon juice, add the garlic and pour evenly over the vegetables. Mix together the cheese and breadcrumbs and sprinkle over the top of the dish. Cook in the microwave for 6 minutes, turning the dish 3 times during cooking. Mix together the chopped hard-boiled eggs and parsley and spoon down the middle of the dish. Serve hot or cold.

Cheesy flowerpot loaves (page 84)

Macaroni cheese de luxe

Utensils: 3.5-litre/6-pint (U.S. 7½-pint) ovenproof mixing bowl. 2.25-litre/4-pint (U.S. 5-pint) ovenproof mixing bowl
Microwave cooking time: 31 minutes

Serves: 4

METRIC/IMPERIAL	AMERICAN
225 g/8 oz macaroni, broken into short lengths	½ lb macaroni, broken into short lengths
generous litre/2 pints hot water	2½ pints hot water
1 teaspoon salt	1 teaspoon salt
50 g/2 oz butter	¼ cup butter
150 g/5 oz onion, finely chopped	1¼ cups finely chopped onion
25 g/1 oz flour	¼ cup all-purpose flour
600 ml/1 pint milk	2½ cups milk
175 g/6 oz Cheddar cheese, grated	1½ cups grated Cheddar cheese
salt and freshly ground black pepper	salt and freshly ground black pepper
paprika pepper	paprika pepper
Garnish:	Garnish:
2 tomatoes, skinned and sliced	2 tomatoes, skinned and sliced
few sprigs parsley	few sprigs parsley

Place the macaroni in the larger mixing bowl with the water and salt. Cook in the microwave for 15 minutes, stirring twice during cooking; drain and rinse.

Melt the butter in the smaller mixing bowl in the microwave for 1 minute, then add the onion and continue to cook in the microwave for 6 minutes. Stir in the flour to absorb the butter then gradually mix in the milk. Add the grated cheese and cook in the microwave for 5 minutes, stirring twice during cooking.

Add the macaroni, season lightly and return to the microwave for 4 minutes, stirring 4 times during cooking.

Transfer to a serving dish, sprinkle with paprika and garnish with tomato slices and parsley before serving.

Potato pizza

Utensils: 1-litre/2-pint (U.S. 2½-pint) round shallow ovenproof dish, 1-litre/2-pint (U.S. 2½-pint) oven-proof pudding basin
Microwave cooking time: 9 minutes

Serves: 4

METRIC/IMPERIAL	AMERICAN
350 g/12 oz mashed potato	1½ cups mashed potato
25 g/1 oz fine dried white breadcrumbs	¼ cup fine dry bread crumbs
1 teaspoon dried mixed herbs	1 teaspoon dried mixed herbs
salt and freshly ground black pepper	salt and freshly ground black pepper
100 g/4 oz onion, chopped	1 cup chopped onion
50 g/2 oz green pepper, chopped	½ cup chopped green pepper
100 g/4 oz streaky bacon, chopped	¼ lb bacon slices, chopped
1 (396-g/14-oz) can tomatoes, drained	1 (14-oz) can tomatoes, drained
175 g/6 oz cheese, grated	1½ cups grated cheese
1 (50-g/1¾-oz) can anchovy fillets	1 (1¾-oz) can anchovy fillets
few black olives	few ripe olives

Mix together the mashed potato, breadcrumbs and herbs. Season lightly and press in the base and slightly up the sides of the round shallow dish.

Mix together the onion, green pepper and bacon in the pudding basin and cook in the microwave for 5 minutes. Arrange this mixture on the potato base. Top with the drained tomatoes and grated cheese. Arrange the anchovy fillets in a lattice pattern on top of the pizza and cook in the microwave for 4 minutes, turning the dish 4 times during cooking. Place an olive in each square of the lattice before serving.

Cheese fondue

Utensil: 1.75-litre/3-pint (U.S. 4-
   pint) earthenware fondue dish
Microwave cooking time:
   6–7 minutes

Serves: 4

METRIC/IMPERIAL	AMERICAN
1 clove garlic	1 clove garlic
150 ml/¼ pint white wine	⅔ cup white wine
1 teaspoon lemon juice	1 teaspoon lemon juice
450 g/1 lb Gruyère or Emmenthal cheese, grated	1 lb Gruyère or Emmenthal cheese, grated
1 tablespoon cornflour	1 tablespoon cornstarch
2 tablespoons brandy	3 tablespoons brandy
pinch freshly ground nutmeg	pinch freshly ground nutmeg
freshly ground black pepper	freshly ground black pepper

Cut the clove of garlic in half and rub the cut sides around the inside of the fondue dish. Pour in the wine and lemon juice and heat in the microwave for 1–2 minutes until just hot. Stir in a third of the cheese, heat in the microwave for 1 minute then repeat with the remaining two-thirds of cheese, adding a third at a time and cook in the microwave for 1 minute in between. After the final amount of cheese has been added return to the microwave for 1 minute, stirring after 30 seconds. Blend the cornflour with the brandy and stir into the fondue. Season to taste and return to the microwave for 2 minutes, stirring frequently. Cool slightly before serving.

Serve with cubes of French bread, celery or florets of cauliflower to dip.

Note: A combination of Gruyère and Emmenthal cheese can be used if preferred.

If a fondue dish is not available, use a suitable casserole dish or a mixing bowl, but remember the cooking times may vary according to the dish used.

Egg custard

Utensils: 600-ml/1-pint (U.S. 2-cup)
   glass measuring jug, 5 150-ml/¼-
   pint (U.S. ⅔-cup) ovenproof
   ramekin dishes, 2.25-litre/
   4-pint (U.S. 5-pint) oblong ovenproof dish
Microwave cooking time:
   11 minutes

Serves: 4–5

METRIC/IMPERIAL	AMERICAN
450 ml/¾ pint milk	2 cups milk
3 eggs	3 eggs
75 g/3 oz sugar	6 tablespoons sugar
few drops vanilla essence	few drops vanilla extract
freshly ground nutmeg	freshly ground nutmeg

Heat the milk in the measuring jug in the microwave for 3 minutes. Add the eggs, sugar and vanilla essence and whisk lightly. Strain and pour into the ramekin dishes. Sprinkle each with a little nutmeg. Stand the dishes in the oblong dish filled with 600 ml/1 pint (U.S. 2½ cups) hand hot water. Cook in the microwave for 8 minutes, turning the large dish and the ramekin dishes 3–4 times during cooking. Leave to cool in the waterbath, then chill in the refrigerator.

Rice and pasta

Rice and pasta may be cooked quickly and easily in the microwave oven, using the normal proportions of liquid. Fill the cooking utensil only half to three-quarters full, for successful results. Small amounts of rice e.g. 100g/4 oz (U.S. ½ cup), are successfully cooked in a 600 ml/1 pint (U.S. 2½ cup) measuring jug. The shape of the jug helps rapid cooking.

During cooking, rice and pasta need only occasional stirring and should be removed from the oven while they are still moist. Since a very high temperature is reached in the food, drying out will continue after removal from the oven, so they should be allowed to stand for a few minutes before serving.

Cooked rice freezes well and may be rapidly defrosted and reheated in the microwave oven. For best results the rice should be frozen in a cook-bag which may then be removed from the freezer, punctured (to allow any steam to escape) and then, discarding any metal clips, placed in the microwave oven to be reheated to serving temperature within minutes.

The type of rice used may alter the cooking time. Most successful are the long-grain varieties which cook by the absorption method. Brown rice may be quickly and successfully cooked in a microwave oven.

Spanish rice

Utensil: 1.75-litre/3-pint (U.S. 4-pints) ovenproof pudding basin
Microwave cooking time: 22 minutes

Serves: 4

METRIC/IMPERIAL
100 g/4 oz onion, chopped
100 g/4 oz streaky bacon, chopped
2 cloves garlic, crushed
175 g/6 oz long grain rice
1 (190-g/6½-oz) can pimientos, drained and chopped
50 g/2 oz button mushrooms, sliced
1 chicken stock cube
450 ml/¾ pint boiling water
50 g/2 oz black olives, stoned
175 g/6 oz tomatoes, skinned and chopped

AMERICAN
1 cup chopped onion
¼ lb bacon slices, chopped
2 cloves garlic, crushed
¾ cup long grain rice
1 (6½-oz) can pimientos, drained and chopped
½ cup sliced mushrooms
1 chicken bouillon cube
2 cups boiling water
⅓ cup pitted ripe olives
6 oz tomatoes, skinned and chopped

Place the onion, bacon and garlic in the pudding basin and cook in the microwave for 5 minutes. Add the rice, pimientos and mushrooms. Dissolve the stock cube in the boiling water and pour over the rice mixture. Stir well and cook in the microwave for 17 minutes or until the rice has absorbed nearly all of the liquid.

Stir in the olives and tomatoes and leave to stand for 3 minutes before serving.

Lamb in onion and caraway sauce (page 53)

Savoury rice ring

Utensils: 2.25-litre/4-pint (U.S. 5-pint) ovenproof mixing bowl, 1.75-litre/3-pint (U.S. 4-pint) round casserole dish
Microwave cooking time: 36–37 minutes

Serves: 4

METRIC/IMPERIAL	AMERICAN
50 g/2 oz butter	¼ cup butter
100 g/4 oz onion, chopped	1 cup chopped onion
100 g/4 oz green pepper, chopped	1 cup chopped green pepper
225 g/8 oz long grain rice	1 cup long grain rice
2 chicken stock cubes	2 chicken bouillon cubes
600 ml/1 pint boiling water	2½ cups boiling water
Filling:	Filling:
50 g/2 oz butter	¼ cup butter
100 g/4 oz red pepper, chopped	1 cup chopped red pepper
100 g/4 oz onion, chopped	1 cup chopped onion
225 g/8 oz raw chicken meat	½ lb raw chicken meat
salt and freshly ground black pepper	salt and freshly ground black pepper
50 g/2 oz button mushrooms	½ cup button mushrooms
juice of 1 orange	juice of 1 orange
2 tablespoons dry sherry	3 tablespoons dry sherry
2 teaspoons cornflour	2 teaspoons cornstarch
2 tablespoons water	3 tablespoons water
Garnish:	Garnish:
1 orange, segmented	1 orange, segmented

Melt the butter in the mixing bowl in the microwave for 2 minutes then add the onion and green pepper and cook in the microwave for a further 4 minutes. Stir in the rice and the stock cubes dissolved in the boiling water. Stir all these ingredients together in the mixing bowl and cook in the microwave for 17 minutes or until the rice is practically dry. Press firmly into a greased 20-cm/8-inch ring mould and chill, overnight preferably.

Melt the butter for the filling in the round casserole in the microwave for 1 minute. Add the red pepper and the onion and cook in the microwave for a further 4 minutes. Roughly shred the raw chicken meat, season lightly and add with the mushrooms to the casserole. Continue to cook in the microwave for 2 minutes, stirring twice. Add the orange juice and sherry and cook for a further 2 minutes, stirring once. Blend the cornflour with the water and stir into the chicken mixture. Thicken in the microwave for 1 minute.

Turn the rice mould on to a serving dish and reheat in the microwave for 3–4 minutes or until fairly hot. Pile the chicken mixture into the centre of the ring and garnish with the orange segments.

Mussel paella

Illustrated on page 23

Utensil: 1.5-litre/2½-pint (U.S. 3-pint) oval ovenproof dish
Microwave cooking time: 19 minutes

Serves: 4

METRIC/IMPERIAL	AMERICAN
1 small onion, finely chopped	1 small onion, finely chopped
½ green pepper, finely chopped	½ green pepper, finely chopped
1 tablespoon oil	1 tablespoon oil
225 g/8 oz long grain rice	1 cup long grain rice
600 ml/1 pint hot chicken stock	2½ cups hot chicken stock
2 tablespoons chopped parsley	3 tablespoons chopped parsley
1 tablespoon chopped chives	1 tablespoon chopped chives
salt and freshly ground black pepper	salt and freshly ground black pepper
2 (150-g/5¼-oz) cans mussels, drained	2 (5¼-oz) cans mussels, drained
3 tomatoes, skinned and chopped	3 tomatoes, skinned and chopped

Place the onion, pepper and oil in the oval dish and cook in the microwave for 5 minutes, stirring once during cooking.

Stir in the rice, chicken stock, parsley, chives and seasoning. Cook in the microwave for a further 10 minutes, stirring after 5 minutes. Add the mussels and tomatoes and heat in the microwave for a further 4 minutes. Remove to a heated serving dish, if liked.

Rice and vegetable salad

Illustrated on page 23

Utensils: 2 1.75-litre/3-pint (U.S. 4-pint) ovenproof basins, 600-ml/ 1-pint (U.S. 2½-cup) glass measuring jug
Microwave cooking time:
  15 minutes: basic rice
  10 minutes: spicy turmeric rice
  22 minutes: brown rice

Serves: 4–6

METRIC/IMPERIAL	AMERICAN
Basic rice:	Basic rice:
225 g/8 oz long grain rice	1 cup long grain rice
600 ml/1 pint hot water (about 65°C/ 150°F)	2½ cups hot water (about 150°F)
1 teaspoon salt	1 teaspoon salt
Spicy turmeric rice:	Spicy turmeric rice:
100 g/4 oz long grain rice	½ cup long grain rice
300 ml/½ pint hot water (about 65°C/ 150°F)	1¼ cups hot water (about 150°F)
¼ teaspoon turmeric	¼ teaspoon turmeric
½ teaspoon salt	½ teaspoon salt
Brown rice:	Brown rice:
100 g/4 oz brown rice	½ cup brown rice
600 ml/1 pint hot water (about 65°C/ 150°F)	2½ cups hot water (about 150°F)
½ teaspoon salt	½ teaspoon salt
Vegetables:	Vegetables:
sliced courgettes, red cabbage, shredded endive, tomato slices, water-cress, shredded white cabbage, peas, grated carrot, cress, sliced aubergine and radishes	sliced zucchini, red cabbage, shredded curly endive, tomato slices, water-cress, shredded white cabbage, peas, grated carrot, cress, sliced eggplant and radishes
Garnish:	Garnish:
sliced hard-boiled egg	sliced hard-cooked egg
soured cream	sour cream
chopped parsley	chopped parsley

Basic rice Place all the ingredients in the basin and cook in the microwave for 15 minutes, stirring 3 times during cooking. Allow to cool.
Spicy turmeric rice Place all the ingredients in the measuring jug and cook in the microwave for 10 minutes, stirring halfway through the cooking time.
Brown rice Place all the ingredients in the basin and cook in the microwave for 22 minutes, stirring every 5 minutes during cooking. Allow to cool.

Serve the cold rice on a large platter, alternating with a selection of prepared vegetables. Garnish with slices of hard-boiled egg and serve with soured cream sprinkled with parsley.

Chicken rice salad

Illustrated on page 14

Utensil: 600-ml/1-pint (U.S. 2½-cup) glass measuring jug
Microwave cooking time:
   10 minutes

Serves: 4

METRIC/IMPERIAL
100 g/4 oz long grain rice
300 ml/½ pint hot water (46°C/115°F)
1 chicken stock cube
225 g/8 oz cooked chicken meat, chopped
1 red pepper, chopped
75 g/3 oz cocktail onions
2 tablespoons capers
grated rind of 1 lemon
2 tablespoons mayonnaise
Garnish:
parsley sprig

AMERICAN
generous ½ cup long grain rice
1¼ cups hot water (115°F)
1 chicken bouillon cube
1 cup chopped cooked chicken meat
1 red pepper, chopped
¾ cup cocktail onions
3 tablespoons capers
grated rind of 1 lemon
3 tablespoons mayonnaise
Garnish:
parsley sprig

Place the rice in the measuring jug together with the water and crumbled stock cube. Cook in the microwave for 10 minutes and leave to stand for 5 minutes.
   Stir the chopped chicken into the rice together with the red pepper, cocktail onions, capers and lemon rind. Leave until cold and mix in the mayonnaise. Turn into a serving dish and garnish with parsley.

Stuffed cannelloni

Utensils: 1-litre/1½-pint (U.S. 2-pint) oblong ovenproof dish, 1.5-litre/2½-pint (U.S. 3-pint) oval ovenproof pie dish
Microwave cooking time:
   19–20 minutes

Serves: 4

METRIC/IMPERIAL
1 small onion, finely chopped
1 tablespoon oil
175 g/6 oz chicken livers, chopped
1 (227-g/8-oz) can tomatoes
225 g/8 oz mushrooms, finely chopped
8 tubes cannelloni
900 ml/1½ pints boiling water
tomato sauce (see page 76)
grated Parmesan cheese

AMERICAN
1 small onion, finely chopped
1 tablespoon oil
6 oz chicken livers, chopped
1 (8-oz) can tomatoes
2 cups finely chopped mushrooms
8 tubes cannelloni
3¾ cups boiling water
tomato sauce (see page 76)
grated Parmesan cheese

Place the onion and oil in the oblong pie dish and cook in the microwave for 3–4 minutes, until the onion is soft. Stir in the chicken livers and continue to cook in the microwave for 3 minutes, stirring once. Add the tomatoes and mushrooms and cook in the microwave for a further 2 minutes.
   Place the cannelloni tubes in the oval dish and pour over the boiling water, making sure the cannelloni is immersed. Cook in the microwave for 10 minutes, stopping half way through the cooking time to rearrange the cannelloni. Drain and stuff each tube with the filling, using a teaspoon. Return the cannelloni to the oval dish. Pour over the tomato sauce, making sure the cannelloni is covered. Sprinkle with Parmesan cheese and reheat in the microwave for 1 minute.

Tipsy kidneys (page 48)

Creamed noodles with mushrooms

Utensils: 1-litre/2-pint (U.S. 2½-
pint) round ovenproof dish, 1.5-
litre/2½-pint (U.S. 3-pint) round
ovenproof dish
Microwave cooking time: 8 minutes

Serves: 4

METRIC/IMPERIAL	AMERICAN
175 g/6 oz ribbon noodles	6 oz ribbon noodles
¼ teaspoon salt	¼ teaspoon salt
450 ml/¾ pint boiling water	2 cups boiling water
100 g/4 oz button mushrooms	1 cup button mushrooms
15 g/½ oz butter	1 tablespoon butter
salt and freshly ground black pepper	salt and freshly ground black pepper
150 ml/¼ pint double cream	⅔ cup heavy cream
Garnish:	Garnish:
poppy seeds	poppy seeds
chopped parsley	chopped parsley

Place the noodles, salt and boiling water in the smaller round dish, cover with cling film and cook in the microwave for 5 minutes, stirring after 3 minutes. Drain and rinse under hot water.

Place the mushrooms and butter in the larger dish and cook in the microwave for 1 minute. Stir in the noodles, seasoning and cream. Heat in the microwave for 2 minutes, stirring once. Garnish with poppy seeds and chopped parsley.

Curried macaroni with nuts

Utensil: 2.25-litre/4-pint (U.S. 5-
pint) ovenproof mixing bowl
Microwave cooking time:
22 minutes

Serves: 4

METRIC/IMPERIAL	AMERICAN
175 g/6 oz cut macaroni	1½ cups cut macaroni
600 ml/1 pint boiling water	2½ cups boiling water
1 teaspoon salt	1 teaspoon salt
25 g/1 oz butter	2 tablespoons butter
1 large onion, chopped	1 large onion, chopped
1 tablespoon curry powder	1 tablespoon curry powder
1 tablespoon flour	1 tablespoon all-purpose flour
2 tablespoons tomato purée	3 tablespoons tomato paste
1 (396-g/14-oz) can tomatoes	1 (14-oz) can tomatoes
100 g/4 oz mushrooms, sliced	1 cup sliced mushrooms
50 g/2 oz sultanas	⅓ cup seedless white raisins
225 g/8 oz salted cashew nuts	2 cups salted cashew nuts
Side dishes:	Side dishes:
½ cucumber, peeled and chopped	½ cucumber, peeled and chopped
1 small carton natural yogurt	1 small carton unflavored yogurt
freshly ground black pepper	freshly ground black pepper
1 red eating apple	1 red eating apple
2 bananas, sliced	2 bananas, sliced
juice of ½ lemon	juice of ½ lemon
2 hard-boiled eggs	2 hard-cooked eggs
2 tomatoes, skinned	2 tomatoes, skinned
few sticks celery	few stalks celery
1 orange, segmented	1 orange, segmented
chopped parsley	chopped parsley

Place the macaroni in the mixing bowl, pour over the boiling water and add the salt. Cook in the microwave for 10 minutes. Allow to stand for 5 minutes before draining.

Using the same mixing bowl, melt the butter in the microwave for 1 minute. Add the onion and curry powder and cook in the microwave for 5 minutes. Stir in the flour then add the tomato purée, tomatoes, mushrooms, sultanas and cashew nuts. Continue to cook for 3 minutes in the microwave, stirring every minute. Stir in the drained macaroni and reheat in the microwave for 3 minutes, stirring 3 times.

To prepare the side dishes

Mix together the cucumber and yogurt and season with freshly ground black pepper. Place in a small dish.

Core and slice the eating apple, mix with the banana and toss in lemon juice to prevent discoloration. Place these in a separate dish.

Quarter the hard-boiled eggs and arrange in a dish with the quartered tomatoes.

Chop the celery and mix with the orange segments. Sprinkle with chopped parsley before serving.

Lasagne

Utensils: 2.25-litre/4-pint (U.S. 5-pint) deep oblong casserole dish, 2.25-litre/4-pint (U.S. 5-pint) ovenproof mixing bowl, 1.75-litre/3-pint (U.S. 4-pint) ovenproof pudding basin
Microwave cooking time:
31 minutes

Serves: 4–6

METRIC/IMPERIAL	AMERICAN
175 g/6 oz lasagne	*6 oz lasagne*
generous litre/2 pints boiling water	*2½ pints boiling water*
1 teaspoon salt	*1 teaspoon salt*
25 g/1 oz butter	*2 tablespoons butter*
1 large onion, chopped	*1 large onion, chopped*
450 g/1 lb spinach, trimmed and chopped	*1 lb spinach, trimmed and chopped*
salt and freshly ground black pepper	*salt and freshly ground black pepper*
Sauce:	Sauce:
50 g/2 oz butter	*¼ cup butter*
4 tablespoons flour	*⅓ cup all-purpose flour*
600 ml/1 pint milk	*2½ cups milk*
175 g/6 oz cheese, grated	*1½ cups grated cheese*
½ teaspoon grated nutmeg	*½ teaspoon grated nutmeg*
450 g/1 lb tomatoes, skinned and sliced	*1 lb tomatoes, skinned and sliced*
Garnish:	Garnish:
tomato slices	*tomato slices*
watercress sprigs	*watercress sprigs*

Place the lasagne in the oblong casserole and pour over the water. Add the salt and cook in the microwave for 10 minutes. Drain the lasagne and dry on kitchen paper.

In the mixing bowl, melt the butter in the microwave for 1 minute then add the onion and cook in the microwave for 3 minutes, stirring once during cooking. Add the spinach and season lightly then continue to cook in the microwave for a further 3 minutes, stirring every minute.

To make the sauce, melt the butter in the pudding basin in the microwave for 2 minutes then stir in the flour. Carefully stir in the milk and season lightly. Cook in the microwave for 7 minutes, stirring 4 times. Add the cheese and nutmeg, taste and adjust the seasoning if necessary.

To assemble the dish, in the deep oblong dish arrange layers of lasagne, spinach, sliced tomatoes and cheese sauce, ending with a layer of sauce on top. Heat the whole dish in the microwave for 5 minutes, turning the dish round 3 times, to reheat evenly. Brown under the grill if liked. Garnish with slices of tomato and sprigs of watercress before serving.

Creamed spaghetti with salami

Utensils: 2.25-litre/4-pint (U.S. 5-pint) deep oblong casserole dish, 2.25-litre/4-pint (U.S. 5-pint) ovenproof mixing bowl
Microwave cooking time: 24 minutes

Serves: 4

METRIC/IMPERIAL	AMERICAN
225 g/8 oz short cut spaghetti	½ lb short cut spaghetti
generous litre/2 pints boiling water	2½ pints boiling water
1 teaspoon salt	1 teaspoon salt
100 g/4 oz onion, thinly sliced	¼ lb onions, thinly sliced
1 clove garlic, crushed	1 clove garlic, crushed
1 tablespoon oil	1 tablespoon oil
1 (198-g/7-oz) can sweetcorn	1 (7-oz) can corn kernels
175 g/6 oz salami, sliced	6 oz salami, sliced
50 g/2 oz button mushrooms, sliced	½ cup sliced mushrooms
100 g/4 oz frozen cut green beans	½ cup frozen cut green beans
150 ml/¼ pint double cream	⅔ cup heavy cream
salt and freshly ground black pepper	salt and freshly ground black pepper

Place the spaghetti in the deep oblong dish, pour over the boiling water and add the salt. Cook in the microwave for 15 minutes and allow to stand in the water for a further 10 minutes before draining and rinsing with boiling water.

Mix the onion, garlic and oil together in the mixing bowl and cook in the microwave for 5 minutes. Add the sweetcorn, salami, mushrooms and green beans, and continue to cook in the microwave for a further 2 minutes, stirring once.

Stir in the cream and season lightly with a little salt and freshly ground black pepper. Heat in the microwave for a further 2 minutes, stirring once and then pour over the drained spaghetti. Toss well and place in a serving dish.

Spaghetti bolognese

Utensils: 2.25-litre/4-pint (U.S. 5-pint) deep oblong casserole, 2.25-litre/4-pint (U.S. 5-pint) ovenproof mixing bowl
Microwave cooking time: 35 minutes

Serves: 4

METRIC/IMPERIAL	AMERICAN
225 g/8 oz short cut spaghetti	½ lb short cut spaghetti
generous litre/2 pints boiling water	2½ pints boiling water
1 teaspoon salt	1 teaspoon salt
25 g/1 oz butter	2 tablespoons butter
225 g/8 oz onion, chopped	2 cups chopped onion
1 green pepper, chopped	1 green pepper, chopped
100 g/4 oz mushrooms, sliced	1 cup sliced mushrooms
450 g/1 lb minced beef	2 cups ground beef
1 clove garlic, crushed	1 clove garlic, crushed
1 (397-g/14-oz) can tomatoes	1 (14-oz) can tomatoes
2 tablespoons tomato purée	3 tablespoons tomato paste
150 ml/¼ pint hot beef stock	⅔ cup hot beef stock
grated Parmesan cheese (optional)	grated Parmesan cheese (optional)

Place the spaghetti in the oblong dish and pour over the boiling water. Add the salt and cook in the microwave for 15 minutes. Leave to stand in the water for 10 minutes before draining and rinsing in boiling water.

Place the butter, together with the onion and green pepper, in the mixing bowl and cook in the microwave for 5 minutes, stirring twice during cooking. Add the mushrooms, minced beef and garlic. Mix together well before stirring in the tomatoes, tomato purée and stock. Cook in the microwave for a further 15 minutes, stirring every 2 minutes. Serve the meat sauce on the spaghetti and sprinkle with a little Parmesan cheese, if liked.

Herby meatballs (page 42)

Pasta shells with seafood salad

Utensils: 1.75-litre/3-pint (U.S. 4-pint) round casserole dish, 1.75-litre/3-pint (U.S. 4-pint) oven-proof pudding basin
Microwave cooking time: 17 minutes

Serves: 4

METRIC/IMPERIAL	AMERICAN
1 (190-g/6½-oz) can tuna in oil	1 (6½ oz) can tuna in oil
1 onion, chopped	1 onion, chopped
1 small green pepper, deseeded and chopped	1 small green pepper, deseeded and chopped
100 g/4 oz button mushrooms, sliced	1 cup sliced mushrooms
2 tablespoons tomato purée	3 tablespoons tomato paste
juice of ½ lemon	juice of ½ lemon
few drops Worcestershire sauce	few drops Worcestershire sauce
225 g/8 oz tomatoes, skinned and chopped	½ lb tomatoes, skinned and chopped
100 g/4 oz cooked mussels	¼ lb cooked mussels
salt and freshly ground black pepper	salt and freshly ground black pepper
175 g/6 oz pasta shells	6 oz pasta shells
900 ml/1½ pints boiling water	3¾ cups boiling water
1 teaspoon salt	1 teaspoon salt
4 tablespoons salad oil	⅓ cup salad oil
2 tablespoons wine vinegar	3 tablespoons wine vinegar
1 teaspoon dried mustard	1 teaspoon dry mustard
½ teaspoon salt	½ teaspoon salt
freshly ground black pepper	freshly ground black pepper
Garnish:	Garnish:
chopped parsley	chopped parsley
lemon twists	lemon twists

Drain the oil from the can of tuna into the round casserole and add the onion and green pepper. Mix well and cook in the microwave for 7 minutes. Add the mushrooms, tomato purée, lemon juice, Worcestershire sauce, tomatoes and mussels. Season well and chill.

Place the pasta shells in the pudding basin and stir in the boiling water and salt. Cook in the microwave for 10 minutes and allow to stand for 5 minutes before draining and rinsing well with cold water. Drain thoroughly and chill.

In a screw-top jar or bottle, shake the remaining ingredients together until emulsified then pour the dressing over the pasta and toss well. Arrange the pasta in a ring on a serving dish and pile the seafood salad in the centre. Sprinkle with a little chopped parsley and garnish with lemon twists before serving.

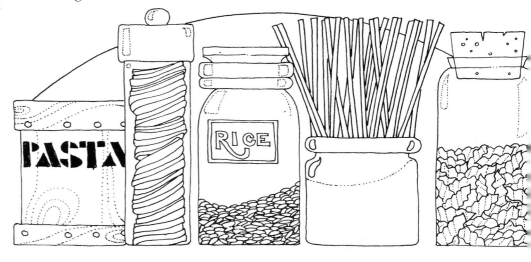

Puddings and desserts

In this chapter the microwave oven shows just how versatile it can be. Whether you want ice cream, cheesecake or Christmas pudding for dessert, there is something here for every taste.

Christmas puddings are no longer the trial they used to be, as the microwave will cook a pudding in only 9 minutes!

Christmas pudding

Utensil: 1-litre/2-pint (U.S. 2½-pint) ovenproof pudding basin
Microwave cooking time: 9 minutes

Serves: 4–6

METRIC/IMPERIAL	AMERICAN
75 g/3 oz butter	6 tablespoons butter
175 g/6 oz currants	1 cup currants
100 g/4 oz raisins	⅔ cup pitted rains
100 g/4 oz sultanas	⅔ cup seedless white raisins
15 g/½ oz almonds, chopped	1 tablespoon chopped almonds
75 g/3 oz plain flour	¾ cup all-purpose flour
pinch mixed spice	pinch mixed spice
pinch nutmeg	pinch nutmeg
75 g/3 oz soft dark brown sugar	6 tablespoons dark brown sugar
2 eggs	2 eggs
rind and juice of 1 lemon	rind and juice of 1 lemon
2 tablespoons black treacle	3 tablespoons molasses
grated rind of 1 orange	grated rind of 1 orange
1 tablespoon brandy	1 tablespoon brandy
gravy browning to colour (optional)	gravy coloring (optional)

Place all the ingredients in a mixing bowl and mix well together. Add a few drops of gravy browning if a dark pudding is preferred. Place in the lightly-greased pudding basin and cover with greased greaseproof paper, securing with an elastic band around the rim. Cook in the microwave for 5 minutes, then allow to stand for 5 minutes. Cook in the microwave for a further 3 minutes and stand for 5 minutes. Finally cook for 1 minute and allow to stand for a few minutes before turning out. Serve hot with brandy sauce (see page 80).

If keeping the pudding, loosely cover with cling film to prevent the surface hardening. When cold, wrap in the greaseproof paper and foil and place in an airtight container.

Note: This pudding will keep for up to 2 months.

Remember, with a microwave Christmas pudding do not add the traditional coin to the mixture!

Scandinavian layer pudding

Utensils: 1.5-litre/2½-pint (U.S. 3-pint) ovenproof soufflé dish, 2.25-litre/4-pint (U.S. 5-pint) ovenproof mixing bowl
Microwave cooking time: 13 minutes

Serves: 4–6

METRIC/IMPERIAL	AMERICAN
100 g/4 oz soft margarine	½ cup soft margarine
100 g/4 oz castor sugar	½ cup sugar
100 g/4 oz hazelnuts, finely chopped	1 cup finely chopped hazelnuts
100 g/4 oz flour	1 cup all-purpose flour
½ teaspoon almond essence	½ teaspoon almond extract
0.75 kg/1½ lb cooking apples	1½ lb baking apples
juice of ½ lemon	juice of ½ lemon
75 g/3 oz castor sugar	6 tablespoons sugar
2 tablespoons water	3 tablespoons water
300 ml/½ pint double cream	1¼ cups heavy cream
4 peaches, stoned and peeled	4 peaches, pitted and peeled

Beat the margarine and sugar until soft and fluffy then beat in the hazelnuts, flour and almond essence. Place the mixture in the soufflé dish and cook in the microwave for 6 minutes, stirring well every 2 minutes. Set aside to cool.

Peel, core and slice the apples and place in the mixing bowl with the lemon juice and sugar. Toss well, add the water and cook in the microwave for 7 minutes until the apples are soft. Stir twice during cooking.

Whip the cream until fairly stiff and reserve a little for decoration. Slice the peaches and reserve a few slices for decoration. Crumble the cooked nut mixture; if necessary this may be placed in a plastic bag and crushed with a rolling pin. Arrange layers of the crumble, apples, peaches and cream in a 1-litre/2-pint (U.S. 2½-pint) glass serving bowl ending with a layer of crumble. Decorate with the reserved whipped cream and peach slices. Serve warm.

Pineapple and ginger layer bombe

Utensil: 1.75-litre/3-pint (U.S. 4-pint) ovenproof pudding basin
Microwave cooking time: 4 minutes

Serves: 4

METRIC/IMPERIAL	AMERICAN
100 g/4 oz soft margarine	½ cup soft margarine
50 g/2 oz castor sugar	¼ cup sugar
2 tablespoons black treacle	3 tablespoons molasses
2 standard eggs	2 medium eggs
100 g/4 oz self-raising flour sifted with 1 teaspoon ground ginger	1 cup all-purpose flour sifted with 1 teaspoon baking powder and 1 teaspoon ground ginger
1 (226-g/8-oz) can pineapple cubes	1 (8-oz) can pineapple cubes
2 tablespoons dry sherry	3 tablespoons dry sherry
300 ml/½ pint double cream	1¼ cups heavy cream
Decoration:	Decoration:
crystallised ginger	candied ginger

Beat together the margarine, sugar and black treacle. Carefully beat in the eggs, one at a time, and fold in the flour and ginger. Line the pudding basin with cling film, transfer the mixture to the pudding basin and cook in the microwave for 4 minutes, turning the dish once. Turn after 2 minutes and cool on a wire tray.

Mix together 2 tablespoons of the canned pineapple juice and the sherry. Split the cake horizontally into 3 layers and soak each piece in the sherry mixture. Whip the double cream until stiff and drain the pineapple cubes. Sandwich together the cake with double cream and pineapple cubes, reserving some cream for covering the cake.

Cover the whole of the outside of the cake with whipped cream and swirl into peaks with a fork.

Decorate with pieces of crystallised ginger.

Chocolate mallow fondue

Utensil: 1.75-litre/3-pint (U.S. 4-pint) ovenproof pudding basin
Microwave cooking time: 3 minutes

Serves: 3–4

METRIC/IMPERIAL
100 g/4 oz plain chocolate
175 g/6 oz marshmallows
1 teaspoon lemon juice

AMERICAN
¼ lb semi-sweet chocolate
6 oz marshmallows
1 teaspoon lemon juice

Place all the ingredients in the pudding basin and melt in the microwave for 3 minutes, stirring after each minute. The chocolate may not have quite melted so allow to stand, stirring occasionally. Serve with cubes of banana, small macaroons and sponge fingers to dip into the fondue.
Note: This fondue is ideal for serving at children's parties, but remember not to serve it too hot.

Compote of cherries

Utensil: 1.5-litre/2½-pint (U.S. 3-pint) oval ovenproof pie dish
Microwave cooking time: 9 minutes

Serves: 4

METRIC/IMPERIAL
450 g/1 lb fresh cherries
4 tablespoons red vermouth
3 tablespoons redcurrant jelly
grated rind and juice of 1 orange

AMERICAN
1 lb fresh cherries
⅓ cup red vermouth
¼ cup red currant jelly
grated rind and juice of 1 orange

Place all the ingredients in the pie dish and cook in the microwave for 9 minutes, stirring twice during cooking. Allow to stand a few minutes before serving. Serve hot with whipped cream.

Banana bake

Illustrated on pages 110–111

Utensil: 1-litre/2-pint (U.S. 2½-pint) oval ovenproof dish
Microwave cooking time: 5 minutes

Serves: 4

METRIC/IMPERIAL
4 bananas, peeled
4 tablespoons undiluted orange juice, thawed
6 tablespoons white wine
1 tablespoon lemon juice
50 g/2 oz brown sugar

AMERICAN
4 bananas, peeled
⅓ cup undiluted orange juice, thawed
½ cup white wine
1 tablespoon lemon juice
¼ cup brown sugar

Slice the bananas in half lengthways then cut each slice in half. Place in the dish and add the remaining ingredients. Cook in the microwave for 5 minutes, stopping halfway to rearrange the fruit (so that the bananas in the centre are moved to the outside of the dish and vice versa). Serve hot with cream.

Caramelised oranges

Utensil: 1-litre/2-pint (U.S. 2½-pint) ovenproof pudding basin
Microwave cooking time: 12 minutes

Serves: 4

METRIC/IMPERIAL
4 large oranges
175 g/6 oz castor sugar
100 ml/4 fl oz cold water
150 ml/¼ pint double cream
1 tablespoon Grand Marnier

AMERICAN
4 large oranges
¾ cup sugar
½ cup cold water
⅔ cup heavy cream
1 tablespoon Grand Marnier

Peel the oranges and remove all the pith. Slice the oranges, remove any pith from the centre and all the pips. Place the slices back together to re-form the orange shape or, alternatively, arrange the slices in a serving dish.

Place the sugar and water in the pudding basin and cook in the microwave for approximately 12 minutes until it becomes a dark golden colour. The caramel may need stirring once or twice during cooking if uneven caramelisation occurs, but this should be avoided if possible. Pour over the oranges.

Chill the oranges overnight in the refrigerator and serve with the cream whipped with the Grand Marnier.

Crunchy apple crisp

Illustrated on pages 110–111

Utensil: oval porcelain flan dish
Microwave cooking time:
  5–7 minutes

Serves: 4

METRIC/IMPERIAL	AMERICAN
3 cooking apples, peeled, cored and sliced	3 baking apples, peeled, cored and sliced
4 tablespoons undiluted orange juice, thawed	$\frac{1}{3}$ cup undiluted orange juice, thawed
75 g/3 oz brown sugar	6 tablespoons brown sugar
50 g/2 oz butter, softened	$\frac{1}{4}$ cup softened butter
175 g/6 oz plain sweet biscuits, crushed	6 oz plain sweet cookies, crushed
Garnish:	Garnish:
orange slices	orange slices

Place the apples evenly on the base of the flan dish and spoon over the orange juice.

Lightly mix together the sugar, butter and crushed biscuits and spoon over the apples. Cook in the microwave for 5–7 minutes, until the apples are soft. Garnish and serve hot with cream.

Note: To thaw frozen orange juice in the microwave, place the frozen juice in a 300-ml/$\frac{1}{2}$-pint (U.S. 1$\frac{1}{4}$-cup) glass measuring jug and place in the microwave for 1 minute. Stir well.

Rhubarb and banana nut crumble

Utensil: 1-litre/1$\frac{1}{2}$-pint (U.S. 2-pint) oblong ovenproof pie dish
Microwave cooking time: 9 minutes

Serves: 4

METRIC/IMPERIAL	AMERICAN
275 g/10 oz rhubarb, trimmed	10 oz rhubarb, trimmed
50 g/2 oz castor sugar	$\frac{1}{4}$ cup sugar
2 bananas	2 bananas
little lemon juice	little lemon juice
Topping:	Topping:
50 g/2 oz butter	$\frac{1}{4}$ cup butter
100 g/4 oz plain flour	1 cup all-purpose flour
50 g/2 oz brown sugar	$\frac{1}{4}$ cup brown sugar
50 g/2 oz toasted hazelnuts, chopped	$\frac{1}{2}$ cup chopped toasted hazelnuts

Slice the rhubarb to approximately 1–2-cm/$\frac{1}{2}$–$\frac{3}{4}$-inch lengths, place in the pie dish and sprinkle with the castor sugar. Cook in the microwave for 5 minutes, stirring twice. Slice the bananas and sprinkle with the lemon juice then mix into the rhubarb mixture.

Rub the butter into the flour until it resembles fine breadcrumbs, then stir in the brown sugar and toasted hazelnuts. Sprinkle evenly over the top of the rhubarb mixture and fork the top lightly.

Cook in the microwave for 4 minutes, turning the dish round once, and leave for a few minutes before serving with whipped cream.

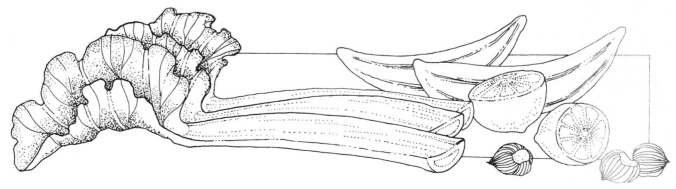

Raspberry mousse

Utensils: 1-litre/2-pint (U.S. 2½-pint) ovenproof pudding basin, 3.5-litre/6-pint (U.S. 7-pint) ovenproof mixing bowl
Microwave cooking time: 14–16 minutes

Serves: 4–6

METRIC/IMPERIAL	AMERICAN
3 eggs, separated	3 eggs, separated
75 g/3 oz castor sugar	6 tablespoons sugar
300 ml/½ pint milk	1¼ cups milk
150 ml/¼ pint double cream	⅔ cup heavy cream
15 g/½ oz gelatine	2 envelopes gelatin
1 tablespoon hot water	1 tablespoon hot water
300 ml/½ pint raspberry purée, sieved	1¼ cups sieved raspberry purée
Decoration:	Decoration:
150 ml/¼ pint double cream, whipped	⅔ cup heavy cream, whipped
chopped nuts	chopped nuts
few whole raspberries	few whole raspberries

Lightly whisk the egg yolks with the sugar then stir in the milk and cream. Pour into the pudding basin. Place the pudding basin in the mixing bowl and pour about 1.5 litre/2½ pints (U.S. 3 pints) boiling water into the bowl to reach the level of the custard in the basin. Cook in the microwave for 14–16 minutes, stirring every 2 minutes for the first 12 minutes, then every minute until the custard will coat the back of a spoon. Cool slightly.

Dissolve the gelatine in the hot water and stir into the raspberry purée. Carefully combine the custard and the purée by very slowly adding the purée to the custard. Chill until half set.

Prepare a 12-cm/5½-inch soufflé dish by tying a double band of grease-proof paper round the edge to come 5 cm/2 inches above the top of the dish. Secure firmly with string. Whisk the egg whites until they form stiff peaks then fold into the half set mousse. Pour into the prepared soufflé dish and chill until set. Carefully remove the greaseproof paper by edging a knife between the paper and the soufflé.

Press the nuts on to the sides of the soufflé and pipe the whipped cream round the edge. Decorate the cream at intervals with whole raspberries.

Pineapple and orange turnabout

Illustrated on pages 110–111

Utensil: 1-litre/2-pint (U.S. 2½-pint) oval ovenproof pie dish
Microwave cooking time: 10–12 minutes

Serves: 4–5

METRIC/IMPERIAL	AMERICAN
1 (226-g/8-oz) can pineapple slices, drained	1 (8-oz) can pineapple slices, drained
glacé cherries	candied cherries
4 tablespoons undiluted orange juice, thawed	⅓ cup undiluted orange juice, thawed
110 g/4 oz soft margarine	½ cup soft margaine
110 g/4 oz castor sugar	½ cup sugar
2 eggs	2 eggs
110 g/4 oz self-raising flour	1 cup all-purpose flour, sifted with 1 teaspoon baking powder
Decoration:	Decoration:
150 ml/¼ pint double cream, whipped	⅔ cup heavy cream, whipped
angelica	candied angelica

Line the dish with cling film and arrange the pineapple slices decoratively on the base. Place a glacé cherry half in the centre of each slice and pour over the orange juice. Place the remaining ingredients in a mixing bowl and beat until well mixed. Spoon over the pineapple, spreading evenly. Cook in the microwave for 10–12 minutes, giving the dish a half turn after the first 5 minutes. Turn out on to a plate and decorate with rosettes of whipped cream and angelica.

Rice crème brûlée

Illustrated opposite

Utensils: 1.75-litre/3-pint (U.S. 4-pint) ovenproof pudding basin, 3.5-litre/6-pint (U.S. 7½-pint) ovenproof mixing bowl
Microwave cooking time: 21½–23½ minutes

Serves: 4–6

METRIC/IMPERIAL	AMERICAN
225 g/8 oz long grain rice, cooked omitting salt (see page 93)	1 cup long grain rice, cooked omitting salt (see page 93)
4 egg yolks	4 egg yolks
2 tablespoons castor sugar	3 tablespoons sugar
300 ml/½ pint single cream	1¼ cups light cream
300 ml/½ pint double cream	1¼ cups heavy cream
175 g/6 oz castor sugar	¾ cup sugar
100 ml/4 fl oz cold water	½ cup cold water
50 g/2 oz toasted whole almonds	½ cup toasted whole almonds

Place the cold, cooked rice in the pudding basin. Lightly whisk together the egg yolks and the 2 tablespoons (U.S. 3 tablespoons) castor sugar, stir in the creams and pour this mixture over the rice. Stir well so that the rice is well mixed.

Place the pudding basin in the mixing bowl and pour 1 litre/2 pints (U.S. 2½ pints) boiling water into the outer dish. Cook in the microwave for 10–12 minutes, stirring twice during the first 5 minutes and then every minute as the custard begins to thicken. Pour the rice custard into a shallow oblong dish and chill thoroughly.

Place the sugar and water into the cleaned pudding basin and cook in the microwave for 11½ minutes or until the sugar caramelises to a dark golden colour. Sprinkle the top of the chilled custard with the almonds and pour over the caramel to evenly cover the surface. Chill thoroughly.

Crème brûlée

Utensils: 1.5-litre/2½-pint (U.S. 3-pint) ovenproof soufflé dish, 2.25-litre/4-pint (U.S. 5-pint) deep oblong ovenproof dish
Microwave cooking time: 12 minutes

Serves: 4

METRIC/IMPERIAL	AMERICAN
4 egg yolks	4 egg yolks
2 tablespoons castor sugar	3 tablespoons sugar
300 ml/½ pint single cream	1¼ cups light cream
300 ml/½ pint double cream	1¼ cups heavy cream
75 g/3 oz soft light brown sugar	6 tablespoons light brown sugar

Lightly whisk together the egg yolks and sugar then stir in the single and double cream. Pour into the soufflé dish and then place the dish in the deep oblong dish.

Fill the larger dish with boiling water up to the level of the custard in the soufflé dish (about 1 litre/2 pints (U.S. 2½ pints)) and cook in the microwave for 12 minutes, turning the soufflé dish 3 times during cooking. Leave to cool.

Place the cooled custard in the refrigerator and chill thoroughly, preferably overnight. Carefully cover the top of the custard with the brown sugar and press down lightly. Place under a preheated grill until the sugar meits and serve immediately.

Spiced pears in mulled wine

Illustrated on the jacket

Utensil: 1.75-litre/3-pint (U.S. 4-
    pint) round ovenproof pie dish
Microwave cooking time: 10 minutes

Serves: 4

METRIC/IMPERIAL	AMERICAN
4 ripe even-sized pears	4 ripe even-sized pears
600 ml/1 pint red wine (or use half water and wine)	2½ cups red wine (or use half water and wine)
pinch nutmeg	pinch nutmeg
1 (5-cm/2-inch) stick cinnamon	1 (2-inch) stick cinnamon
50 g/2 oz sugar	¼ cup sugar
pared rind of ½ lemon	pared rind of ½ lemon
few drops lemon juice	few drops lemon juice
4 cloves	4 cloves

Peel the pears, leaving whole with the stalks on. Place the remaining ingredients in the pie dish and cook in the microwave for 5 minutes. Carefully place the pears in the hot wine and return to the microwave for a further 5 minutes. Leave to stand for 5 minutes before serving.

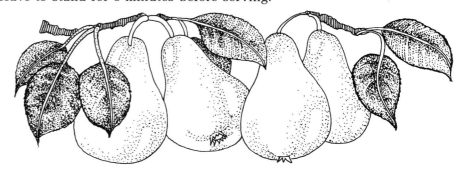

Grapefruit cheesecake

Illustrated on pages 110–111

Utensils: 1-litre/2-pint (U.S. 2½-pint)
    ovenproof basin, 20-cm/8-inch
    china flan dish
Microwave cooking time:
    4½ minutes

Serves: 4–6

METRIC/IMPERIAL	AMERICAN
50 g/2 oz butter	¼ cup butter
125 g/4 oz digestive biscuits, crushed	1½ cups graham cracker crumbs
175 g/6 oz cream cheese	¾ cup cream cheese
2 eggs, lightly whisked	2 eggs, lightly whisked
pinch salt	pinch salt
75 g/3 oz castor sugar	6 tablespoons sugar
3 tablespoons undiluted grapefruit juice, thawed	¼ cup undiluted grapefruit juice, thawed
vanilla essence to taste	vanilla extract to taste
almond essence to taste	almond extract to taste
100 ml/4 fl oz soured cream	½ cup sour cream
Decoration:	Decoration:
150 ml/¼ pint double cream, whipped	⅔ cup heavy cream, whipped
grapefruit segments	grapefruit segments

Place the butter in the basin and melt in the microwave for 30 seconds. Stir in the crushed biscuit crumbs and mix well. Press into the flan dish, lining the base and sides evenly.

Lightly whisk the remaining ingredients together until well blended and smooth. Pour into the flan dish and cook in the microwave for 2 minutes, turning the dish after 1 minute. Cook in the microwave for a further minute, turning after 30 seconds. Allow to stand for 1 minute, then return to the microwave for 1 minute, turning after 30 seconds. Allow to cool, then chill in the refrigerator.

Decorate with whipped cream and grapefruit segments.

Variation

Use undiluted orange juice in place of the grapefruit juice.

Apple, apricot and almond sponge

Utensils: 1.75-litre/3-pint (U.S. 4-pint) ovenproof pudding basin, 2.25-litre/4-pint (U.S. 5-pint) ovenproof mixing bowl, 1-litre/2-pint (U.S. 2½-pints) oblong ovenproof pie dish
Microwave cooking time: 43 minutes (see note)

Serves: 4–6

METRIC/IMPERIAL	AMERICAN
225 g/8 oz dried apricots	½ lb dried apricots
600 ml/1 pint cold water	2½ cups cold water
450 g/1 lb cooking apples, peeled, cored and sliced	1 lb baking apples, peeled, cored and sliced
25 g/1 oz castor sugar	2 tablespoons sugar
50 g/2 oz soft margarine	¼ cup soft margarine
50 g/2 oz castor sugar	¼ cup sugar
1 egg	1 egg
25 g/1 oz self-raising flour	¼ cup all-purpose flour sifted with
½ teaspoon baking powder	¾ teaspoon baking powder
25 g/1 oz ground almonds	¼ cup ground almonds
50 g/2 oz toasted flaked almonds	½ cup toasted slivered almonds

Place the dried apricots with half the water in the pudding basin and cook in the microwave for 20 minutes, stirring 3 times. Add the remaining water and continue to cook in the microwave for a further 12 minutes, stirring twice.

Add the apples to the drained apricots in the mixing bowl and cook in the microwave for 5 minutes, stirring once. Transfer to the pie dish.

Place the margarine, sugar, egg, flour, baking powder and almonds in a mixing bowl and whisk thoroughly to give a light fluffy consistency. Spread this mixture over the fruit in the pie dish and sprinkle the toasted almonds over the top. Cook in the microwave for 6 minutes, turning the dish 3 times during cooking. Serve with whipped cream.

Note: For a quicker alternative, used drained canned apricots and omit the first 32 minutes cooking time.

Crème caramel

Utensils: 1-litre/2-pint (U.S. 2½-pint) ovenproof pudding basin, 4 150-ml/¼-pint (U.S. ⅔-cup) ovenproof ramekin dishes, 2.25-litre/4-pint (U.S. 5-pint) deep oblong ovenproof dish
Microwave cooking time: 16½ minutes

Serves: 4

METRIC/IMPERIAL	AMERICAN
Caramel:	Caramel:
6 tablespoons castor sugar	½ cup sugar
3 tablespoons hand hot water (about 48°C/120°F)	4 tablespoons hand hot water (about 120°F)
Custard:	Custard:
2 eggs	2 eggs
1½ tablespoons castor sugar	2 tablespoons sugar
450 ml/¾ pint milk	2 cups milk

Mix the sugar and water for the caramel together in the pudding basin and cook in the microwave for approximately 8 minutes or until the caramel turns a dark golden colour. It might be necessary to stir the caramel once during cooking if uneven browning occurs. Coat the base and insides of each ramekin with the caramel and set aside to cool.

Lightly whisk together the eggs and sugar for the custard and stir in the milk. Pour the custard into the ramekin dishes and place them in the oblong dish. Pour almost boiling water in the dish to surround the ramekins up to the level of the custard. Cook in the microwave for 8½ minutes, turning the large dish and ramekin dishes 3–4 times during cooking, until the custards are lightly set – they will become more firm on chilling.

Place the custards in a refrigerator to chill, preferably overnight. When required, turn out and serve with whipped cream.

Banana bake (page 103), Grapefruit cheesecake (page 108), Crunchy apple crisp (page 104) and Pineapple and orange turnabout (page 105)

Vanilla ice cream

Utensil: 1.75-litre/3-pint (U.S. 4-pint) round ovenproof dish
Microwave cooking time: 6 minutes

Serves: 4

METRIC/IMPERIAL	AMERICAN
2 eggs, whisked	2 eggs, whisked
450 ml/¾ pint milk	2 cups milk
175 g/6 oz castor sugar	¾ cup sugar
1 tablespoon vanilla essence	1 tablespoon vanilla extract
300 ml/½ pint double cream	1¼ cups heavy cream

Combine the eggs, milk and sugar in the round dish and cook in the microwave for 6 minutes, stirring frequently. Allow to cool, then stir in the vanilla essence and cream. Pour into a freezing tray or a rigid shallow plastic container and freeze until semi-solid. Whisk again and return to the freezer. Allow to thaw at room temperature for 1–2 hours before serving.

Orange and apricot ice cream

Utensils: 600-ml/1-pint (U.S. 2½-cup) glass measuring jug, 2 1.75-litre/3-pint (U.S. 4-pint) oven-proof mixing bowls
Microwave cooking time:
    14–15 minutes

Serves: 6–8

METRIC/IMPERIAL	AMERICAN
1 (178-ml/6½-fl oz) can frozen orange juice	1 (6½-fl oz) can frozen orange juice
225 g/8 oz dried apricots	½ lb dried apricots
2 eggs	2 eggs
450 ml/¾ pint milk	2 cups milk
175 g/6 oz sugar	¾ cup sugar
300 ml/½ pint double cream	1¼ cups heavy cream

Place the orange juice in the measuring jug and melt in the microwave for 1–2 minutes. Add sufficient water to make up to 600 ml/1 pint (U.S. 2½ cups). Pour into the mixing bowl with the apricots and leave to soak for 1 hour.

Whisk the eggs, milk and sugar together in the second mixing bowl and cook in the microwave for 5 minutes, stirring during cooking. Allow to cool.

Cook the orange juice and apricots in the microwave for 8 minutes, stirring once, and allow to cool. Stir the cream into the egg mixture, pour into a shallow rigid plastic container and partially freeze.

Liquidise the orange juice and apricots into a purée and stir into the partially frozen ice cream. Freeze for 1 hour, whisk and then freeze until solid. Allow to thaw for 1–2 hours at room temperature before serving.

Preserves

Preserving is just another exciting aspect of microwave cookery, whether it be jams, chutneys or relishes.

No more messy, sticky saucepans or hot steamy kitchens to contend with; simply cook in an ovenproof mixing bowl, as stated in the recipe.

A jar of preserve is always a nice gift, and with a microwave oven it can be made quickly and easily without fuss.

To sterilise jars in the microwave oven. Half-fill each jar with water and heat in the microwave until boiling. Remove carefully as the jars will be hot, pour off the water and drain upside down for a few minutes before filling.

Testing for setting point of jam made in the microwave oven. There are two ways to test jams or jellies for setting point.

(a)   Place a small spoonful of the jam on a saucer and allow to become cold. If it wrinkles when pushed with a finger, setting point has been reached.

(b)   Stir with a wooden spoon and hold horizontally until a firm drip appears.

Whilst doing these tests, remove the jam or jelly from the microwave, as it may become overcooked.

Plum jam

Illustrated on pages 118–119

Utensil: 1.75-litre/3-pint (U.S. 4-pint) ovenproof mixing bowl
Microwave cooking time:
*   21 minutes*

Makes: about 1 kg/2 lb

METRIC/IMPERIAL	AMERICAN
0.75 kg/1½ lb plums, stoned and quartered	1½ lb plums, pitted and quartered
450 g/1 lb castor sugar	1 lb sugar

Place the plums in the mixing bowl and cook in the microwave for 5 minutes, stirring once. Stir in the sugar until completely dissolved. Return to the microwave and cook for 16 minutes or until the jam has reached setting point. Stir several times during cooking. Allow to cool slightly before bottling in sterilised jars. Cover with circles of waxed paper, seal and label.

Redcurrant and apple jam

Illustrated on pages 118–119

Utensil: 2.25-litre/4-pint (U.S. 5-pint) ovenproof mixing bowl
Microwave cooking time:
*   28–33 minutes*

Makes: about 1.25 kg/2½ lb

METRIC/IMPERIAL	AMERICAN
450 g/1 lb redcurrants	1 lb red currants
300 ml/½ pint water	1¼ cups water
350 g/12 oz cooking apples, peeled, cored and sliced	12 oz baking apples, peeled, cored and sliced
1 kg/2 lb castor sugar	2 lb sugar

Place the redcurrants and water in the mixing bowl and cook in the microwave for 3 minutes. Stir in the apples and continue to cook in the microwave for 5 minutes.

Add the sugar and stir until dissolved. Return to the microwave and cook for a further 20–25 minutes, stirring occasionally during cooking, until the jam has reached setting point. Bottle in sterilised jars, cover with circles of waxed paper, seal and label.

Sweet orange marmalade

Illustrated on pages 118–119

Utensil: 1.75 litre/3-pint (U.S. 4-pint) ovenproof mixing bowl
Microwave cooking time:
  25 minutes

Makes: about 0.75–1 kg/1½–2 lb

METRIC/IMPERIAL	AMERICAN
2 large oranges	2 large oranges
1 lemon	1 lemon
300 ml/½ pint boiling water	1¼ cups boiling water
450 g/1 lb castor sugar	1 lb sugar

Coarsely grate the rind from the oranges and lemon. Cut the fruit into small pieces and place in the mixing bowl with the grated rinds and water. Cook in the microwave for 5 minutes. Add the sugar and stir until completely dissolved.

Return to the microwave and cook for 20 minutes or until setting point is reached. Stir twice during cooking.

Allow to cool slightly before bottling in sterilised jars. Cover with circles of waxed paper, seal and label.

Apple jelly

Illustrated on pages 118–119

Utensil: 2.25-litre/4-pint (U.S. 5-pint) ovenproof mixing bowl
Microwave cooking time:
  33 minutes

Makes: about 1 kg/2 lb

METRIC/IMPERIAL	AMERICAN
50 g/2 oz castor sugar	¼ cup sugar
6 tablespoons commercial pectin	½ cup commercial pectin
750 ml/1¼ pints apple juice	3 cups apple juice
450 g/1 lb castor sugar	1 lb sugar
few drops lemon juice	few drops lemon juice
few drops Angostura bitters	few drops Angostura bitters

Place the sugar, pectin and apple juice in the mixing bowl and stir well. Cook in the microwave for 5 minutes, stirring once during cooking. Add the 450 g/ 1 lb sugar and stir until dissolved. Return to the microwave and cook for 28 minutes, stirring at 5-minute intervals, until a temperature of 96–98°C/205–210°F is reached, or when stirred with a wooden spoon and held horizontally a firm drop appears. Stir in a few drops of lemon juice and Angostura bitters. Bottle in sterilised jars. Cover with circles of waxed paper, seal and label. Keep in a cool place.

Apple butter

Illustrated on pages 118–119

Utensil: 2.25-litre/4-pint (U.S. 5-pint) ovenproof mixing bowl
Microwave cooking time:
  15 minutes

Makes: about 1 kg/2 lb

METRIC/IMPERIAL	AMERICAN
1 kg/2 lb cooking apples, peeled, cored and sliced	2 lb baking apples, peeled, cored and sliced
25 g/1 oz butter	2 tablespoons butter
90 g/3⅓ oz sugar	7 tablespoons sugar
pinch cinnamon	pinch cinnamon
few cloves	few cloves
150 ml/¼ pint water	⅔ cup water

Place all the ingredients in the mixing bowl and cook in the microwave for 15 minutes, stirring at 5-minute intervals. Remove the cloves, then mash the apple mixture until creamy. Bottle the apple butter in sterilised jars. Cover with circles of waxed paper, seal and label.
Note: Keep in the refrigerator for up to 3 weeks only.

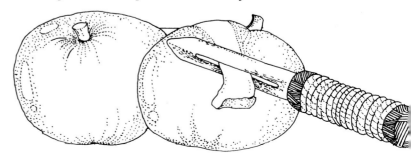

Blackberry ketchup

Illustrated on pages 118–119

Utensils: large cook-bag, 3-litre/
5-pint (U.S. 6½-pint) ovenproof
mixing bowl
Microwave cooking time:
25 minutes

Makes: about 1 litre/1½ pints (U.S.
2 pints)

METRIC/IMPERIAL	AMERICAN
350 g/12 oz onions, chopped	3 cups chopped onion
1 kg/2 lb frozen blackberries	2 lb frozen blackberries
150 ml/¼ pint vinegar	⅔ cup vinegar
½ teaspoon salt	½ teaspoon salt
1 tablespoon sugar	1 tablespoon sugar
1 teaspoon mustard	1 teaspoon mustard
pinch ground cloves	pinch ground cloves
freshly ground black pepper	freshly ground black pepper

Place all the ingredients in the large cook-bag and secure loosely with an elastic band. Place the bag of ingredients in the mixing bowl and cook in the microwave for 25 minutes, rearranging the ingredients in the bag every 5 minutes.

Liquidise the mixture then cool it and press through a sieve. Place in clean, sterilised screw-top or clip-top bottles and store in the refrigerator for up to one month.

Tomato and apple relish

Utensils: 600-ml/1-pint (U.S. 2½-
cup) glass measuring jug, cook-
bag 2.25-litre/4-pint (U.S. 5-pint)
ovenproof mixing bowl
Microwave cooking time:
38–43 minutes

Makes: about 0.75–1 kg/1½–2 lb

METRIC/IMPERIAL	AMERICAN
200 ml/7 fl oz malt or wine vinegar	¾ cup malt or wine vinegar
1 teaspoon pickling spice	1 teaspoon pickling spice
1 kg/2 lb tomatoes, peeled and chopped	2 lb tomatoes, peeled and chopped
1 cooking apple, peeled, cored and sliced	1 baking apple, peeled, cored and sliced
1 small onion, finely chopped	1 small onion, finely chopped
salt and freshly ground black pepper	salt and freshly ground black pepper
225 g/8 oz castor sugar	1 cup sugar
pinch ground ginger	pinch ground ginger

Place the vinegar and pickling spice in the measuring jug and heat in the microwave for 2 minutes, then strain.

Place the tomatoes, apple and onion in the cook-bag, securing loosely with an elastic band. Cook in the microwave for 6 minutes, stopping after 3 minutes to rearrange the tomatoes, apple and onion, taking care to avoid the steam.

Carefully turn into the mixing bowl with the strained vinegar, salt, pepper and sugar. Continue to cook in the microwave for 30–35 minutes, until reduced. Stir in the ginger to taste. Bottle in sterilised jars, cover with circles of waxed paper, seal and label.

Cranberry relish

Illustrated on pages 118–119

Utensil: 1.75-litre/3-pint (U.S. 4-
pint) ovenproof mixing bowl
Microwave cooking time:
10 minutes

Makes: about 350 g/12 oz

METRIC/IMPERIAL	AMERICAN
275 g/10 oz cranberries	2½ cups cranberries
1 tablespoon concentrated unsweetened orange juice	1 tablespoon concentrated unsweetened orange juice
2 tablespoons wine vinegar	3 tablespoons wine vinegar
75 g/3 oz castor sugar	6 tablespoons sugar

Place the cranberries, orange juice and vinegar in the mixing bowl and cook in the microwave for 5 minutes, stirring once during cooking.

Gently mash the fruit and stir in the sugar. Return to the microwave and cook for 5 minutes.

Bottle in a sterilised jar, cover with a circle of waxed paper, seal and label. Serve with poultry, game and gammon.

Piccalilli

Illustrated on pages 118–119

Utensils: 1-litre/2-pint (U.S. 2½-pint) ovenproof pudding basin, cook-bag, 600-ml/1-pint (U.S. 2½-cup) glass measuring jug, 2.25-litre/4-pint (U.S. 5-pint) ovenproof mixing bowl
Microwave cooking time: 28 minutes

Makes: about 1.5 kg/3 lb

METRIC/IMPERIAL	AMERICAN
225 g/8 oz cucumber, cubed	2 cups diced cucumber
225 g/8 oz green tomatoes, chopped	½ lb green tomatoes, chopped
225 g/8 oz onions, sliced	½ lb onions, sliced
225 g/8 oz shallots, peeled and left whole	½ lb shallots, peeled and left whole
225 g/8 oz cauliflower florets	½ lb cauliflower florets
225 g/8 oz celery, chopped	2 cups chopped celery
generous litre/2 pints water	2½ pints water
25 g/1 oz salt	2 tablespoons salt
25 g/1 oz flour	¼ cup all-purpose flour
2 teaspoons dry mustard	2 teaspoons dry mustard
¼ teaspoon turmeric	¼ teaspoon turmeric
75 g/3 oz sugar	6 tablespoons sugar
Spiced vinegar:	Spiced vinegar:
600 ml/1 pint malt vinegar	2½ cups malt vinegar
blade mace	blade mace
few peppercorns	few peppercorns
few cloves	few cloves
pinch allspice	pinch allspice
pinch cinnamon	pinch cinnamon
pinch chilli powder	pinch chili powder

Place all the vegetables in a large bowl, cover with the water and salt. Cover and leave overnight.
For the spiced vinegar, place the vinegar and all the spices in the pudding basin and heat in the microwave for 8 minutes, stirring once. Allow to cool.

Drain and rinse the vegetables and place in the cook-bag. Lightly secure the cook-bag with an elastic band and cook in the microwave for 5 minutes.

Mix the flour, mustard, turmeric and sugar with a little of the spiced vinegar to a smooth paste. Pour the remaining spiced vinegar into the glass measuring jug and heat in the microwave for 2 minutes, until hot. Pour on to the blended flour, stir and return to the jug and cook in the microwave for a further 2 minutes.

Place the cooked vegetables in the mixing bowl and pour over the vinegar mixture. Cook in the microwave for 11 minutes, stirring twice during cooking. Allow to stand before bottling in sterilised jars. Cover with a circle of waxed paper, seal and label.

Green tomato chutney

Illustrated on pages 118–119

Utensils: 600-ml/1-pint (U.S. 2½-cup) glass measuring jug, 2.25-litre/4-pint (U.S. 5-pint) ovenproof mixing bowl
Microwave cooking time: 30 minutes

Makes: about 0.75 kg/1½ lb

METRIC/IMPERIAL	AMERICAN
100 g/4 oz onion, finely chopped	1 cup finely chopped onion
300 ml/½ pint vinegar	1¼ cups vinegar
450 g/1 lb green tomatoes, skinned and chopped	1 lb green tomatoes, skinned and chopped
2 apples, peeled, cored and chopped	2 apples, peeled, cored and chopped
½ teaspoon dry mustard	½ teaspoon dry mustard
pinch ground ginger	pinch ground ginger
pinch salt	pinch salt
100 g/4 oz sultanas	⅔ cup seedless white raisins
100 g/4 oz castor sugar	½ cup sugar

Place the chopped onion in the measuring jug with half the vinegar. Cover with cling film and cook in the microwave for 5 minutes. Transfer to the mixing bowl and add the tomatoes, apple, mustard, ginger, salt and sultanas. Cover and cook in the microwave for 10 minutes, stirring frequently.

Stir in the sugar and the remaining vinegar. Return to the microwave and cook for a further 15 minutes, stirring once during cooking.

Bottle in sterilised jars, seal and label.

Rhubarb chutney

Utensil: 3-litre/5-pint (U.S. 6½-pint) oblong casserole dish
Microwave cooking time:
    30 minutes

Makes: about 1 kg/2 lb

METRIC/IMPERIAL	AMERICAN
450 g/1 lb rhubarb, sliced	1 lb rhubarb, sliced
50 g/2 oz raisins	⅓ cup pitted raisins
50 g/2 oz sultanas	⅓ cup seedless white raisins
few cloves	few cloves
4 onions	4 onions
150 g/5 oz soft brown sugar	⅔ cup soft brown sugar
pinch mustard	pinch mustard
pinch salt	pinch salt
grated rind of 1 orange	grated rind of 1 orange
450 ml/¾ pint vinegar	2 cups vinegar

Place all the ingredients in the casserole dish and cook in the microwave for 30 minutes, stirring every 5 minutes.

Bottle the chutney while still hot in sterilised jars. Cover the chutney with circles of waxed paper, seal and label.

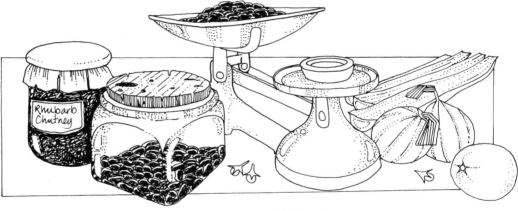

Gooseberry chutney

Utensils: cook-bag, 1.75-litre/3-pint (U.S. 4-pint) ovenproof mixing bowl
Microwave cooking time:
    27 minutes

Makes: about 0.5 kg/1 lb

METRIC/IMPERIAL	AMERICAN
450 g/1 lb gooseberries, topped and tailed	1 lb gooseberries, stemmed
225 g/8 oz onions, finely chopped	2 cups finely chopped onion
salt and freshly ground black pepper	salt and freshly ground black pepper
150 ml/¼ pint white vinegar	⅔ cup white vinegar
1 teaspoon pickling spice, tied in a muslin bag	1 teaspoon pickling spice, tied in a cheesecloth bag
175 g/6 oz castor sugar	¾ cup sugar

Place the gooseberries and onions in the cook-bag, securing loosely with an elastic band. Cook in the microwave for 7 minutes, stopping after 3 minutes to rearrange the gooseberries.

Carefully turn out into the mixing bowl and stir in the remaining ingredients. Cook in the microwave for 20 minutes until reduced. Remove the bag of pickling spice and bottle in sterilised jars. Cover with circles of waxed paper, seal and label.

Menus and time plans

When cooking a complete meal in the microwave oven, timing needs to be very carefully planned, to allow the dishes to be separately cooked, yet still be piping hot and ready to eat when required.

Complete breakfast for 1
Total microwave cooking time = 4¼ minutes
Sausage, egg, tomato and bacon
(see page 122) — 2 minutes
Roll and butter
(see chart page 123) — 15 seconds
Coffee
(see chart page 123) — 2 minutes

ADVANCE PREPARATION
Place all the food on a plate and cover, either the previous night or just before cooking.
Note: If the food has been refrigerated overnight the microwave cooking time will need to be increased.

WHEN REQUIRED
Cook the food on the plate in the microwave.
Heat the roll and then the coffee in the microwave.

Luncheon for 4
Total microwave cooking time = 11–13 minutes
Scotch eggs in herby cheese sauce
(see page 84) — 6 minutes
Green salad
Crunchy apple crisp
(see page 104) — 5–7 minutes

ADVANCE PREPARATION
Hard-boil eggs and coat. Prepare the remaining ingredients.
Prepare and assemble the salad.
Prepare and assemble the Crunchy apple crisp.

WHEN GUESTS ARRIVE
Cook the Scotch eggs in the microwave.
Make the sauce and finish the dish. Serve.
Whilst eating the main course cook the dessert in the microwave.
Leave to stand for a few minutes before serving.

Luncheon for 4
Total microwave cooking time = 24 minutes
Mussel paella
(see page 92) — 19 minutes
Green salad
Banana bake
(see page 103) — 5 minutes

ADVANCE PREPARATION
Prepare and assemble the salad.
Prepare ingredients for the paella.
Make and assemble the Banana bake.

WHEN GUESTS ARRIVE
Cook paella in the microwave.
Whilst eating the main course cook the Banana bake in the microwave and leave to stand before serving.

Dinner party for 4
Total microwave cooking time = 61 minutes
Grapefruit with vermouth
(see page 27) — 2 minutes
Rolled galantine of chicken
(see page 56)—20 minutes
Lyonnaise potatoes
(see page 65) — 15 minutes
Courgettes
(see chart page 72) — 3 minutes
Crème caramel
(see page 109) — 16½ minutes
Coffee
(see chart page 123) — 4½ minutes

ADVANCE PREPARATION

Prepare and cook the Crème caramel the previous day and chill overnight.
Bone and stuff the chicken.
Prepare the grapefruit.
Prepare the vegetables for the Lyonnaise potatoes and cook the onions in the microwave. Arrange the onions and potatoes in layers in the dish.

WHEN GUESTS ARRIVE

Cook the stuffed chicken in the microwave and stand for 15 minutes. Whilst the chicken is standing . . . pour the cream over the potatoes and cook in the microwave for 5 minutes, remove and allow to stand whilst cooking the grapefruit.
Return the potatoes to the microwave and continue with the cooking time.
Serve the grapefruit.
Remove the potatoes from the microwave and cook the courgettes whilst slicing the chicken.
Heat the coffee in the microwave

Fondue party for 4
Total microwave cooking time = 10¼–11¼ minutes
Cheese fondue
(see page 89) — 6–7 minutes
Garlic bread
(see chart page 123) — 1 minute 15 seconds (for 1 French loaf, cut in half)
Fruity mulled wine
(see page 122) — 3 minutes

ADVANCE PREPARATION

Make up the garlic bread.
Grate cheese and prepare ingredients for the fondue.
Prepare the ingredients for the mulled wine.

WHEN GUESTS ARRIVE

Heat the mulled wine in the microwave and allow to cool slightly before serving. Cook the fondue in the microwave. Allow to cool slightly whilst heating the garlic bread.
Serve the fondue with a selection of dippers, such as carrot sticks, cauliflower florets, apple slices, etc.

Breakfast

METRIC/IMPERIAL
2 rashers streaky bacon
2 chipolata sausages
1 egg
1 tomato

AMERICAN
2 bacon slices
2 link sausages
1 egg
1 tomato

Utensils: 150-ml/¼-pint (U.S. ⅔-cup)
 ovenproof ramekin dish, 23-cm/
 9-inch round ovenproof plate
Microwave cooking time: 2 minutes

Serves: 1

Wrap the bacon rashers around the sausages and place on the plate. Butter the ramekin dish, break in the egg and stand on the plate. Add the halved tomato. Cook in the microwave for 2 minutes, turning the dish once.
Note: Cooking for 2 minutes produces an egg with a slightly soft yolk. If a very soft egg is required, the ramekin dish should be placed on the plate after 30 seconds cooking time.

Apple toddy

METRIC/IMPERIAL
1 (929-ml/32.7-fl oz) jar concentrated
 apple juice
1 orange, studded with cloves
1 (5-cm/2-inch) stick cinnamon
freshly ground nutmeg
3 tablespoons Calvados

AMERICAN
1 (32.7-fl oz) jar concentrated apple
 juice
1 orange, studded with cloves
1 (2-inch) stick cinnamon
freshly ground nutmeg
¼ cup Calvados

Utensil: 2.25-litre/4-pint (U.S. 5-pint)
 ovenproof mixing bowl
Microwave cooking time: 8 minutes

Serves: 6

Place the ingredients in the mixing bowl and heat in the microwave for 8 minutes, stirring once during cooking. Carefully remove the orange and discard the cloves. Slice the orange and float on top of the toddy. Serve hot.

Fruity mulled wine

METRIC/IMPERIAL
1 bottle dry red wine
finely pared rind of 1 lemon
finely pared rind of 1 orange
juice of 1 lemon
juice of 1 orange
2 tablespoons clear honey
300 ml/½ pint port
4 cloves
few slices orange and lemon

AMERICAN
1 bottle dry red wine
finely pared rind of 1 lemon
finely pared rind of 1 orange
juice of 1 lemon
juice of 1 orange
3 tablespoons clear honey
1¼ cups port
4 cloves
few slices orange and lemon

Utensil: 1.75-litre/3-pint (U.S. 4-pint)
 mixing bowl
Microwave cooking time: 3 minutes

Serves: 6

Pour the wine into the mixing bowl, add the lemon and orange rinds and juices. Stir in the honey and port, add the cloves and heat in the microwave oven for 3 minutes. Remove the fruit rinds and cloves, and add the orange and lemon slices just before serving.

Warming spicy wine

METRIC/IMPERIAL
1 bottle dry red wine
6 lumps sugar (or to taste)
6 cloves
small piece root ginger
¼ teaspoon cinnamon
150 ml/¼ pint brandy
little grated nutmeg

AMERICAN
1 bottle dry red wine
6 cubes sugar (or to taste)
6 cloves
small piece ginger root
¼ teaspoon cinnamon
⅔ cup brandy
little grated nutmeg

Utensil: 1.75-litre/3-pint (U.S. 4-pint)
 mixing bowl
Microwave cooking time: 3½ minutes

Serves: 6

Pour the wine into the mixing bowl and add the sugar, cloves, ginger and cinnamon. Heat in the microwave oven for 3½ minutes then remove the ginger and cloves. Stir in the brandy and sprinkle over grated nutmeg before serving.

Convenience foods cooking chart_____

Food	Quantity or weight	Cooking utensil	Amount of cooking liquid	Microwave cooking time	Special instructions
DRIED FOODS					
Apple flakes	35-g/1¼-oz packet 225 g/8 oz reconstituted	1-litre/2-pint (U.S. 2½-pint) ovenproof pudding basin	300 ml/½ pint (U.S. 1¼ cups) cold water	3 minutes	Stir 3 times
Apricots	225 g/8 oz	1.75-litre/3-pint (U.S. 4-pint) ovenproof pudding basin	600 ml/1 pint (U.S. 2½ cups) cold water	30 minutes	Stir 4 times
Beans, butter (soaked)	225 g/8 oz	2.25-litre/4-pint (U.S. 5-pint) ovenproof mixing bowl	1 litre/2 pints (U.S. 2½ pints) boiling water	45 minutes	Stir 3 times
Beans, haricot (soaked)	225 g/8 oz	2.25-litre/4-pint (U.S. 5-pint) ovenproof mixing bowl	1 litre/2 pints (U.S. 2½ pints) boiling water	40 minutes	Stir 4 times
Beans, green (quick dried)	32-g/1.1-oz packet	1.75-litre/3-pint (U.S. 4-pint) ovenproof pudding basin	900 ml/1½ pints (U.S. 3¾ cups) cold water	10 minutes	Stir twice
Beans, red (soaked)	225 g/8 oz	2.25-litre/4-pint (U.S. 5-pint) ovenproof mixing bowl	1 litre/2 pints (U.S. 2½ pints) boiling water	45 minutes	Stir 4 times
Onions, sliced (quick-dried)	40-g/1.4-oz packet	1-litre/2-pint (U.S. 2½-pint) ovenproof pudding basin	450 ml/¾ pint (U.S. 2 cups) cold water	5 minutes	—
Peas, dried (soaked)	225 g/8 oz	2.25-litre/4-pint (U.S. 5-pint) ovenproof mixing bowl	1 litre/2 pints (U.S. 2½ pints) boiling water	50 minutes	Add ½ teaspoon salt after 40 minutes
Peas (quick-dried)	113-g/4-oz packet	1.75-litre/3-pint (U.S. 4-pint) ovenproof pudding basin	900 ml/1½ pints (U.S. 3¾ cups) cold water	13 minutes	Stir 3 times
Peas, split	225 g/8 oz	2.25-litre/4-pint (U.S. 5-pint) ovenproof mixing bowl	1 litre/2 pints (U.S. 2½ pints) boiling water	40 minutes	Stir 4 times
Prunes (unsoaked)	225 g/8 oz	1-litre/2-pint (U.S. 2½-pint) ovenproof pudding basin	450 ml/¾ pint (U.S. 2 cups) boiling water	20 minutes	Stir 4 times

Convenience foods cooking chart

Food	Quantity or weight	Cooking utensil	Amount of cooking liquid	Microwave cooking time	Special instructions
SAUCES AND SOUPS (packet mixes, dried)					
Apple sauce	28 g/1 oz	1-litre/2-pint (U.S. 2½-pint) ovenproof pudding basin	200 ml/⅓ pint (U.S. ¾ cup) cold water	3 minutes	Stir twice
Onion sauce	28 g/1 oz	600-ml/1-pint (U.S. 2½-cup) glass measuring jug	300 ml/½ pint (U.S. 1¼ cups) milk	4 minutes	Stir 4 times
Asparagus soup	57 g/2 oz	1.75-litre/3-pint (U.S. 4-pint) ovenproof pudding basin	600 ml/1 pint (U.S. 2½ cups) cold water	6 minutes	Whisk 3 times
Spring vegetable soup	28 g/1 oz	1.75-litre/3-pint (U.S. 4-pint) ovenproof pudding basin	600 ml/1 pint (U.S. 2½ cups) cold water	10 minutes	Whisk 4 times
FROZEN FOODS					
Purchased					
Bread, rolls	2	kitchen paper	—	1 minute*	—
Bread, sliced	2 slices	kitchen paper	—	1 minute*	Turn over once
Chips, crinkle cut (cooked)	100 g/4 oz	1-litre/2-pint (U.S. 2½-pint) ovenproof pudding basin	—	2 minutes	Rearrange once
Cod, in butter sauce	170 g/6 oz	boil-in-bag	—	5 minutes	Pierce bag before cooking to allow steam to escape
Fish cakes	4 (225 g/8 oz)	large square rigid plastic microwave dish	—	4 minutes	Turn fish cakes over and round once
Orange juice, frozen	178-ml/6½-fl oz can	transferred to 300-ml/½-pint (U.S. 1¼-cup) glass measuring jug	—	1 minute*	Stir once
Peas	450 g/1 lb	in the bag purchased in	—	8 minutes	Pierce bag to allow steam to escape
Pork chops	2 thick ones (2 cm/¾ inch thick)	polystyrene tray	—	3 minutes	Turn chops once. Resting time 15 minutes
Strawberries	225 g/8 oz	round flat ovenproof dish	—	2 minutes*	Rearrange fruit once

*Microwave defrosting time

Food	Quantity or weight	Cooking utensil	Amount of cooking liquid	Microwave cooking time	Special instructions
Home-made cooked dishes					
Bread, garlic	½ French loaf (175 g/6 oz)	double thickness kitchen paper	—	1½ minutes	—
Casserole, beef	4 servings	round strong plastic dish	—	10 minutes	Break up the block of casserole as it thaws
Cottage pie	4 servings	oblong rigid plastic microwave dish	—	15 minutes	Remove dish from oven after 10 minutes. Cover with foil and rest for 5 minutes. Remove foil and cook for a further 5 minutes
Cheesecake	2 pieces (175 g/6 oz)	oblong strong plastic lid	—	30 seconds*	—
Complete meal: meat patties new potatoes peas gravy	2 (100 g/4 oz) 4 (150 g/5 oz) 100 g/4 oz 4 tablespoons	oblong rigid plastic microwave dish	—	8 minutes	Turn dish 4 times
Meat patties (raw)	4 (225 g/8 oz)	large square rigid plastic microwave dish	—	6 minutes	Turn patties over and round 3 times
Rice, long-grain, cooked	450 g/1 lb	in heavy weight polythene bag	—	8 minutes	Pierce bag to allow steam to escape
Sauces and soups					
Bolognese sauce	4 servings	place block in 1-litre/ 2-pint (U.S. 2½-pint) oblong ovenproof dish	—	12 minutes	Break up the block as it defrosts
Onion sauce	300 ml/½ pint (U.S. 1¼ cups)	1-litre/2-pint (U.S. 2½-pint) ovenproof pudding basin	—	4 minutes	Break up the block as it defrosts
Apple sauce	150 ml/¼ pint (U.S. ⅔ cup)	small solid plastic dish	—	3 minutes	—
Cauliflower soup	1 litre/2 pints (U.S. 2½ pints)	place block in cook-bag	—	18 minutes	Place the cook-bag in a large bowl to prevent spillage

*Microwave defrosting time

Convenience foods cooking chart

Food	Quantity or weight	Cooking utensil	Amount of cooking liquid	Microwave cooking time	Special instructions
REHEATING FOODS					
Bread, rolls	2	kitchen paper	—	30 seconds	—
Complete meal	(see frozen meal)	plain white round plate in cook-bag	—	3 minutes	—
Meat and potato pie (with pastry crust)	individual size	small round plate	—	1 minute	—
Steak and kidney pudding	individual size	upturned on small round plate	—	3 minutes	—
MISCELLANEOUS					
Coffee, instant	1 teaspoon	300-ml/½-pint (U.S. 1¼-cup) mug	250 ml/scant ½ pint (U.S. 1 cup) cold water	2 minutes	Stir once
Gravy mix	3 heaped teaspoons	600-ml/1-pint (U.S. 2½-cup) glass measuring jug	300 ml/½ pint (U.S. 1¼ cups) cold water	3 minutes	Whisk well twice
Jelly, orange	127-g/4½-oz tablet	600-ml/1-pint (U.S. 2½-cup) glass measuring jug	300 ml/½ pint (U.S. 1¼ cups) cold water	3½ minutes	Stir twice Make up to 600 ml/ 1 pint (U.S. 2½ cups) with cold water
Porridge	100 g/4 oz	1.75-litre/3-pint (U.S. 4-pint) ovenproof pudding basin	600 ml/1 pint (U.S. 2½ cups) cold water ¼ teaspoon salt 2 tablespoons sugar	5 minutes	Stir twice
Potato, instant	127-g/4½-oz packet	2.25–litre/4-pint (U.S. 5-pint) ovenproof mixing bowl	600 ml/1 pint (U.S. 2½ cups) cold water 25 g/1 oz (U.S. 2 tablespoons) butter	4 minutes	Stir twice
Soya granules high protein e.g. Mince Savour	60-g/2⅛-oz packet	1-litre/2-pint (U.S. 2½-pint) ovenproof pudding basin	150 ml/¼ pint (U.S. ⅔ cup) cold water	1¼ minutes	Stir once
Spaghetti	40 g/1½ oz	600-ml/1-pint (U.S. 2½-cup) glass measuring jug	300 ml/½ pint (U.S. 1¼ cups) cold water	3 minutes	Stir 3 times
Sponge cake mix	184-g/6½-oz packet	1.5-litre/2½-pint (U.S. 3-pint) ovenproof soufflé dish	2 eggs	3 minutes	Turn dish 3 times. Resting time 3 minutes (after cooking)

Index

127

Index